Revolutions in World History

Revolutions have been a part of politics for centuries. Their ideologies, their leaders, and their successes or failures have shaped the history of nations worldwide. This comparative survey focuses on five major case studies, beginning with the English revolutions in the seventeenth century, and continuing with the Mexican, Russian, Vietnamese, and Iranian revolutions.

Revolutions in World History traces the origins, developments, and outcomes of these revolutions, providing an understanding of the revolutionary tradition in a global context. The study raises questions about motivations and ideologies. In particular, it examines the effectiveness of these revolutions – and revolution as a concept – in bringing about lasting political changes.

Michael D. Richards is Samford Professor of History at Sweet Briar College, Virginia. His previous publications include *Twentieth Century Europe: A Brief History* and *Europe, 1900–1980*, and he writes on occasion for the History News Service.

Themes in World History
Series editor: Peter N. Stearns

The *Themes in World History* series offers focused treatment of a range of human experiences and institutions in the world history context. The purpose is to provide serious, if brief, discussions of important topics as additions to textbook coverage and document collections. The treatments will allow students to probe particular facets of the human story in greater depth than textbook coverage allows, and to gain a fuller sense of historians' analytical methods and debates in the process. Each topic is handled over time – allowing discussions of changes and continuities. Each topic is assessed in terms of a range of different societies and religions – allowing comparisons of relevant similarities and differences. Each book in the series helps readers deal with world history in action, evaluating global contexts as they work through some of the key components of human society and human life.

Revolutions in World History

Michael D. Richards

Routledge
Taylor & Francis Group

NEW YORK AND LONDON

First published 2004
by Routledge
270 Madison Ave, New York, NY 10016

Simultaneously published in the UK
by Routledge
2 Park Square, Milton Park, Abingdon, Oxon, OX14 4RN

Routledge is an imprint of the Taylor & Francis Group

Reprinted 2005

Transferred to Digital Printing 2010

Typeset in Garamond by
Keystroke, Jacaranda Lodge, Wolverhampton

Library of Congress Cataloging in Publication Data
Richards, Michael D.
Revolutions in world history / Michael D. Richards.
   p. cm. – (Themes in world history)
1. Revolutions–History. 2. Revolutions–Case studies. I. Title. II. Series.
  JC491.R497 2003
   303.6′4′0903–dc22   2003020464

British Library Cataloguing in Publication Data
A catalogue record for this book is available from the
British Library

ISBN 0–415–22497–7 (hbk)
ISBN 0–415–22498–5 (pbk)

Contents

Acknowledgments

Over the years Peter N. Stearns has generously afforded me several opportunities to write about revolutions and their impact in history. It is a particular pleasure to continue that association by participating in the "Themes in World History" series edited by Professor Stearns.

I want to thank all those at Routledge who have helped turn my initial outline into a book. I begin with the very patient Victoria Peters, Senior Editor. Ruth Whittington, Production Editor, and Colin Morgan, Project Manager, have also been most helpful.

Sweet Briar College has supported me in two ways. For many years now, it has allowed me to teach "Revolutions in the Modern World." In 2003 the administration kindly made it possible for me to spend two weeks traveling in Vietnam and Cambodia, seeing for myself many of the sites of the Vietnamese Revolution.

Molly Kalkstein, a superb editor with whom I have worked on several other projects, gave the entire manuscript a careful and most helpful reading. Her comments and suggestions were enormously useful.

Finally, I want to acknowledge the support and help of Dr. Nancy Dutton Potter. She insisted, quite rightly, that I rethink and rewrite the introduction. Her insightful questions helped me do that. Naturally, neither she nor anyone else I have mentioned bears responsibility for any errors of infelicities that may yet remain.

Michael D. Richards
Sweet Briar, Virginia
8 December 2003

Chapter 1

Bringing revolutions back into history

World history is filled with coups, revolts, and rebellions. It offers, by way of contrast, relatively few revolutions. The first is arguably the Dutch Revolt against the Spanish crown, beginning in the late sixteenth century. This book attempts to put revolutions back into history. It does this by examining the role of revolutions in world history from the seventeenth century through the twentieth century. To accomplish this goal, it makes use of comparative studies of the seventeenth-century British revolutions and twentieth-century revolutions in Mexico, Russia, Vietnam, and Iran.

Three propositions have guided the comparative study of the five revolutions. The first asserts that political repertoires have included the phenomenon of revolution since the seventeenth century. Put another way, revolutions became at some point in the seventeenth century one way of doing politics, one way of deciding who paid what price to accomplish certain ends.

The second proposition is that the use of power is more important than the seizure of power. Obviously the seizure of power is a prerequisite to its use and of considerable interest, but one cannot claim to fully understand a revolution without studying its life course. If this book has some claim to originality, it lies in the idea that revolutions go well beyond the seizure and consolidation of power. They may be episodic or segmented, as was, for example, the Russian Revolution. The events of the 1930s, the Stalin Revolution, might be considered a second and much more convulsive part of the 1917 revolution. It is, in fact, difficult to say where a revolution ends. It becomes embedded in the history of a nation, constantly used or misused in contemporary politics.

Thirdly, whether revolutions ever are completely finished, there are criteria by which a revolution may be considered a "success" or a "failure." Such a proposition is inherently controversial in that it seems to rest on a highly subjective evaluation. Nevertheless, there are a few criteria that, applied to a particular revolution, may lead to an objective assessment of that revolution. A "successful" revolution, then, should do the following: (1) it should provide for individual liberty; (2) it should result in a flexible and open political system that can deal with economic, social, and cultural changes; and (3) it should generate improvement in the well-being of those it affects.

The phenomenon of revolution is best understood in historical terms. The comparative studies that follow occupy a middle ground between the study of individual revolutions, the approach of many historians, and overarching theories that explain the dynamics of revolution, an approach taken mostly by political scientists and sociologists.

Some time ago, I advanced the idea of "clusters of revolution," as in the Atlantic revolutions of the late eighteenth century, the revolutions of 1848 in Europe or the several revolutions between 1900 and 1920 in what might be called semi-colonial countries (Russia, Persia, Mexico, China). Looking at clusters of revolutions offers a good approach to the task of recognizing broad patterns. At the same time, it is still important to insist that geographical locations and cultural traditions make a difference even when the revolutions are contemporaneous and subject to similar environmental factors. The search for patterns, for typologies, is useful in dealing with what is otherwise a jumble of detail. Ultimately, however, the useful insights derived from these efforts must be anchored in the historical details of a particular revolutionary experience.

It is also important to understand that the concept of revolution has its own history. Anyone thinking about revolution in the early years of the twenty-first century cannot help but think about it differently from the way someone thought about it early in the twentieth century. Events in Russia, China, Vietnam, the German Democratic Republic and elsewhere in the past century have changed the way people view revolutions. Revolutionaries themselves often have a historical perspective, hoping to find in the past lessons or answers they can use.

At this point, a definition of revolution is probably overdue. At a minimum, revolution involves the use of or the threat of the use of force either to recover a political system that appears to have been eroded or to bring into being a new political system. In many cases, revolution also involves the creation of different social or economic arrangements. In some cases, it may even entail thorough going cultural change.

It would be all too easy to get lost in the thickets of theory, but, as is the case with a working definition of the revolution, a brief theoretical orientation is also useful. The year 1979 was a good one for revolutions. It featured not only two very different revolutions in Iran and in Nicaragua but also publication of a groundbreaking book by Theda Skocpol, *States and Social Revolution*. A review of the literature since the publication of *States and Social Revolution* makes it clear that Skocpol's ideas, somewhat modified in response to critics, have continued to exert extraordinary influence down to the present (it is interesting to note a kind of lineage in that Skocpol was a student of Barrington Moore, Jr., a major contributor to comparative studies of revolution, and that one of her students, Jeff Goodwin, has emerged as a major figure in comparative studies in his own right).

I take from Skocpol's work primarily the emphasis on the state as an autonomous actor, both on the domestic level and on the international. For there to be a chance of revolution the state must, inadvertently of course, create a potentially revolutionary situation. This may involve a fiscal crisis, as in the case of France in 1789, or a regime that fails to maintain an adequate coalition of elites, as in the case of Mexico in 1910.

Some group, or perhaps a coalition of groups, then has to respond to the potentially revolutionary situation. The would-be revolutionaries may already have been in existence before the situation developed or may have found each other only after the appearance of new possibilities. Charles Tilly's work, in *From Mobilization to Revolution* among others, has been helpful in understanding how revolutionaries organize and locate necessary resources.

Although class-based analyses have grown increasingly sophisticated, they nonetheless do more to obscure the dynamics of revolutions than to clarify them. And, also problematic, they reinforce a tendency to concentrate on the origins of revolution. As a graduate student, I read Georges Lefebvre's brilliant study of 1789, published in English as *The Coming of the French Revolution: 1789*, which laid out the role of each class in the revolution very convincingly: an aristocratic revolution providing an opening, a bourgeois revolution creating a national assembly and beginning the work of drafting a constitution, a popular revolution and then a peasant revolution protecting and extending the initial efforts, all of these streams coming together in the "Declaration of the Rights of Man and Citizen" in August and in the October days that led the revolutionaries and the royal family from Versailles back to Paris. In the end, however, Lefebvre's analysis, brilliant and convincing as it was, was simply too schematic to reflect the complicated opening months of the revolution.

Finally, culture matters. In 1981 I arranged a panel on "States and Social Revolution" for the annual meeting of the American Historical Association. One of the panelists, William Sewell, contributed a long paper, later published in the *Journal of Modern History* with a rejoinder by Skocpol. Without taking sides in that very fruitful debate between Sewell and Skocpol, I will note that it made me aware of just how much culture mattered. Emiliano Zapata's role in the Mexican Revolution furnishes one example of the power of culture. In 1909 he was elected president of the village council of Anenecuilco. At the age of thirty, he had already proved himself an able defender of village rights. Although Zapata was not a peasant and had never worked as a day laborer on the hacienda, he was nonetheless regarded as a man of the people. Understanding the problems of his own village and the many other similar villages in the state of Morels made him a formidable leader in the Mexican Revolution. His inability to see the larger national picture, however, meant that eventually he would lose out to revolutionaries with wider perspectives.

Because of the need to bring revolutions back into history, this book begins with an examination of the British Revolution of the seventeenth century rather than the French Revolution of the eighteenth century. The former reveals in a striking manner the ways in which revolution is simply another way of doing politics. It is worth noting that the people involved in revolutions in Britain in the 1640s and 1650s and again in 1688 only reluctantly changed the existing political system. Change, in fact, was disguised as the recovery or the preservation of old rights and institutions.

In France the revolution appeared first as a response to the contemporary political situation, but it soon became, in effect, an attempt to escape from history, to start over. It was, to be sure, a very different approach to politics, perhaps stretching the idea of politics to its limit. Nonetheless, even in France and the subsequent revolutions that aimed at beginning afresh, revolution was still an integral part of politics.

Whether revolution builds on existing institutions and procedures or attempts to make a fresh start, it must be seen as part of the historical process. Sometimes, in the life of a society or nation, as the title of a recent book on revolutions by Jeff Goodwin has it, there is *No Other Way Out* of a particular situation than through revolution. There are costs involved in dealing with any situation where politics comes into play. Politics is essentially a process for determining who pays, how much, and in what manner to accomplish the desired goal.

The Cold War produced an obsession with the origins of revolution. The reasoning was that if it were possible to understand what caused revolutions, it might be possible to find ways to prevent them from occurring. To some extent, we have moved from an over-emphasis on the origins of revolution and the seizure of power to a concern with the use of power. In any case, beginning with the British Revolutions of the seventeenth century also helps us see the importance of taking a long-term view of the phenomenon of revolution.

Until we have seen how revolutionaries put power to use it is difficult to determine whether a revolution has succeeded or failed, Of course, a revolution that does not result in the seizure of power is clearly a failure even though it may leave a legacy, as was, for example, the case with the 1905 Revolution in Russia. It is possible that the "failure" of a revolution may create conditions leading to its eventual "success." In the case of the British Revolution of the 1640s and 1650s, the restoration of the Stuart kings in the person of Charles II seemed to mark the mid-century revolutionary efforts as a failure. The Stuart dynasty, however, ran into problems, to which the Revolution of 1688 formed one possible solution. Over an additional period of more than a century, an evolutionary process, with occasional near-revolutionary situations, led to the development of a constitutional monarchy with the House of Commons as its political center – a successful and enduring political system.

Once the idea of revolution became part of the political repertoire, even if many political actors did not care to acknowledge it as such, individuals and groups tried with increasing frequency to make use of it. The nineteenth century is filled with efforts, mostly unsuccessful, to imitate the French Revolution of 1789. Several of these efforts took place in France itself, as the French seemed doomed to repeat their initial revolutionary experience.

Ultimately, the revolutions of the nineteenth century demonstrated the *historical character* of revolution. Revolution in the nineteenth century was mostly about politics, although with the social question and even some ideas about cultural change thrown in. In the course of the nineteenth century, the world changed fundamentally as industrial capitalism and the concept of nation states took hold. Revolution, defined as a form of politics, changed if for no other reason than political problems and political aspirations changed. The addition of economic and social issues complicated the situation even more. Expectations about what a revolution might accomplish increased rapidly.

After the French Revolution, with its idea of starting over, many revolutionaries paradoxically attempted to go outside politics, in a sense to escape from history, by destroying the old regime and setting in its place something with no connections to the old systems, culture, and traditions. The Pol Pot regime in Cambodia in the 1970s provides an extreme example of a desire to set in place a utopian system in which all revolutionaries will be good and pure.

The British Revolutions of the seventeenth century set the stage for the book, calling attention both to the wish to modify and the desire to establish something radically different. The British Revolutions also point to the importance of looking at the use of power and at ways in which "failure" might eventually lead to "success." Finally, the British Revolutions had an impact on other countries and on political thought more generally.

The four remaining chapters focus on twentieth-century revolutions: the Mexican, Russian, Vietnamese, and Iranian revolutions. The Mexican Revolution was the first major revolution of the twentieth century, beginning in 1910 and continuing for most of that decade. It, too, is an excellent illustration of the themes of the book. For example, revolution as an integral part of history, another plausible form of politics, is connected with the failure of the *Porfiriato*, the regime of Porfirio Díaz, to maintain a viable political system. It is perhaps uncharitable to call a regime that lasted thirty-four years a failure; nonetheless, its collapse in 1910 opened the way to revolution. The second concerns the use of power. Tracing that theme requires an examination of the course of Mexican history not only in the revolutionary decade but also through the 1920s and 1930s as well. Out of the turmoil of revolution came a remarkably stable, quite cynical political system that lasted nearly the rest of the century. It was, to be sure, a highly limited system in that it worked well only for certain groups, but it became more successful, at least in its own terms, than one would have predicted in the 1920s. Ultimately, the "success" or "failure" of the Mexican Revolution will depend on the direction taken by Mexico in the next few decades.

The Russian Revolution must count as the most important revolutionary upheaval of the twentieth century. The trauma of World War I led directly to the February Revolution and eventually, also, to the October Revolution. Vladimir Lenin's brand of Marxism also played a crucial role, helping to create the conditions that made the October Revolution possible. Revolution continued to be an alternate method of politics, but now was seemingly a far more consciously directed alternate method.

What makes the Russian Revolution, specifically the "Great October Socialist Revolution," such a powerful component of world history in the twentieth century is that the Soviet Union, operating more and more as a modern variant of the Russian Empire, had the potential to become a major power and did. Lenin seemingly showed the way to seize and retain power. Stalin, his disciple and successor, made it his life's work to turn a weak, backward, largely agricultural country into an industrialized, technologically advanced, and militarily strong nation. After World War II and victory over Nazi Germany offered a validation of the Soviet approach, the Soviet model was almost irresistibly attractive to emerging nations around the world. Marxism–Leninism, as interpreted by Stalin, became the revolutionary ideology of choice.

Marxism–Leninism marked the Vietnamese Revolution as well but so did nationalism and patriotism. Including the Vietnamese Revolution in this book provides an opportunity to examine a national liberation movement of extraordinary duration and persistence. The combination of Marxism and nationalism served to mobilize hundreds of thousands of Vietnamese for extraordinary sacrifices over long periods. Again, the Vietnamese Revolution demonstrates party leaders' increasingly conscious direction of revolutionary efforts.

From another vantage point, the Vietnamese Revolution demonstrates the limits of power. The United States, as successor to the French in Indochina, found it could not create, much less sustain, a South Vietnam that could compete with the Marxist, nationalist regime to the north. Vietnam became in many respects the Spain of the 1960s and 1970s, a cockpit in which great ideologies, this time Democracy and Communism, competed. As was the case with Spain in the 1930s, Vietnam suffered a national tragedy, from which it has not yet fully recovered even though the war of national liberation ended nearly thirty years ago. The United States, although comparatively untouched by its losses in that war, had to contend with a deep psychological wound and the loss of a sense of historical exceptionalism.

The Iranian Revolution in a sense brings us back to the Mexican Revolution. Like the Mexican Revolution, it was, first, a failure of the regime, although the activities of the Ayatollah Khomeini and other religious leaders contributed to the disintegration of the shah's Iran. Religious ideology, in this case militant Islam, became a key element in the Iranian Revolution. It furnished the means for mobilizing large numbers of opposition in Tehran and other cities. It also provided a powerful critique of the shah's policies and program. The international Cold War context, in particular the role of the United States in Iranian affairs, was an important aspect, too.

The Iranian Revolution appeared to be eminently exportable in the sense that Islamic fundamentalism gained an audience not only in the Middle East but also in North Africa and in Central Asia. This portability is an example of another prominent feature of revolution from the time of the French Revolution. While the British Revolution had repercussions, particularly in the idea of a constitutional monarchy in which parliament predominated, from the French Revolution onwards many observers viewed revolution as a kind of contagious disease. The Russian Revolution produced what amounted to a series of crusades against it, and the Vietnamese Revolution produced the "domino" theory, the idea that victory by the Communists in Vietnam would lead to neighboring countries falling, like dominoes lined up in a row, to Communism. While Iran did little to export its revolution, observers often linked it with other Islamic fundamentalist movements.

It is too early to characterize the Iranian Revolution as either a "failed" or a "successful" revolution. Nonetheless, revolutions that construct rigid political, social, and economic systems soon after the seizure of power appear to be good candidates for failure in the long run. The Russian Revolution, for example, even though it underwent what might be seen as a second revolution – the "Stalin Revolution" in the 1930s – developed relatively inflexible patterns that caused it to fall further and further behind its competitors in the West in the 1970s and 1980s and, finally, to implode in 1991.

In summary, the book will discuss in the context of five revolutions – the British in the seventeenth century, and the Mexican, Russian, Vietnamese, and Iranian in the twentieth century, the following basic assertions about revolution:

- A revolution is an integral part of politics, an essential element of history.
- A revolution involves not only the seizure but also the use of power; it can be best understood by studying it over its life course.
- A revolution is more likely to "succeed" if it involves modifications, even if extensive, of systems that existed before the revolution – starting completely anew increases the chance of "failure."

It is, of course, easy to make a series of abstract pronouncements, quite another matter to build a convincing case for them. The following discussion of five revolutions in different time periods and various parts of the world will attempt to provide illustrations and evidence that will help to make a convincing case for the statements above. It will also contribute to an understanding of the historical character of revolutions. While there are, for example, some similarities between the British experience in the seventeenth century and the Iranian experience in the twentieth, there are many more differences because of the significantly different historical circumstances.

We cannot foresee whether the twenty-first century will witness as many revolutions as did the twentieth century. We may have passed the point where an easy faith in social engineering prevails, which could mean fewer people willing to risk revolution. Still, given the number of desperate people in the world and countries in which societies and economies are unraveling because of AIDS or civil war or environmental pressures, there may in fact be more revolutions than ever. Likely there will also be many pseudo-revolutions, regimes that use the rhetoric of revolution to mobilize support or to disguise the actual poverty of their efforts.

A clearer understanding of the phenomenon of revolution should prove valuable as this century continues. In any case, the world we live in today has been and will continue to be shaped by revolutions and their legacies. The mere existence of the phenomenon and the possibility of its reoccurrence is enough to produce some change and reform. To state the obvious, we cannot begin to understand the present or prospects for the future without factoring in the impact of revolution in world history.

Finally, if the study of revolution warns us against the dangers of wholesale change in political, economic, and social structures, it should also warn us against complacency in the face of pressing political and social problems. Politics is still a major aspect of history and it continues to be largely about who pays for what takes place and who benefits. Revolutions provide one way of answering these questions.

Further reading

Brinton, Crane (1965) *The Anatomy of Revolution*, revised and expanded edition. New York: Vintage.

Dunn, John (1972) *Modern Revolutions*. New York: Cambridge University Press.

Foran, John (editor) (1997) *Theorizing Revolutions*. London and New York: Routledge.

Goldstone, Jack A. (1991) *Revolution and Rebellion in the Early Modern World*. Berkeley and Los Angeles: University of California Press.

—— (editor) (1993) *Revolutions: Theoretical, Comparative, and Historical Studies*, second edition. San Diego: Harcourt Brace Jovanovich.

Goldstone, Jack A., Gurr, Ted Robert, and Moshiri, Farrokh (editors) (1991) *Revolutions of the Late Twentieth Century*. Boulder, CO: Westview Press.

Goodwin, Jeff (2001) *No Other Way Out: State and Revolution, 1945–91*. Cambridge: Cambridge University Press.

Keddie, Nikki (editor) (1995) *Debating Revolutions*. New York: New York University Press.

Kimmel, Michael (1990) *Revolution: A Sociological Interpretation*. Philadelphia: Temple University Press.

Lefebvre, George (1947) *The Coming of the French Revolution: 1789*. Princeton, NJ: Princeton University Press.

Moore, Barrington, Jr. (1966) *Social Origins of Dictatorship and Democracy: Lord and Peasant in the Making of the Modern World*. Boston: Beacon Press, 1966.

—— (1978) *Injustice: The Social Bases of Obedience and Revolt*: White Plains, NY: M. E. Sharpe.

Paige, Jeffery M. (1975) *Agrarian Revolution: Social Movements and Export Agriculture in the Underdeveloped World*. New York: Free Press.

Skocpol, Theda (1979) *States and Social Revolutions: A Comparative Analysis of France, Russia, and China.* Cambridge: Cambridge University Press.

—— (1994) *Social Revolutions in the Modern World.* Cambridge: Cambridge University Press.

Tilly, Charles (1978) *From Mobilization to Revolution.* Reading, MA: Addison-Wesley.

—— (1993) *European Revolutions, 1492–1992.* Oxford: Blackwell.

Wickham-Crowley, Timothy P. (1991) *Exploring Revolution: Essays on Latin American Insurgency and Revolutionary Theory.* Armonk, NY: M. E. Sharpe.

Chapter 2

The British Revolution
of the seventeenth century

What many historians now call the British Revolution – the events of
the 1640s and 1650s in the British Isles – others still refer to as the English
Revolution or the English Civil War. Some would see it as a mere rebellion,
others as a political crisis that got out of hand. It was all these and more. The
argument put forth in this chapter is that the events of this period, especially
when considered with the Revolution of 1688, constitute a revolution, probably the first true revolution in world history. Rather than scrap the existing
political system for something altogether new, as happened in so many subsequent revolutions, the English attempted to preserve time-honored customs
and rights. Nonetheless, they succeed over time in creating something new.

England is at the center of the British Revolution. Events in Scotland
and Ireland had importance in and of themselves, of course, but mainly because
of their impact on the revolutionary situation in England. Taken all together,
events in Britain helped to change world history.

While historians no longer see the revolution as a long, self-conscious defense
of English political rights against royal tyranny, people from all levels of society
nonetheless took political issues quite seriously in the 1620s and 1630s. None,
perhaps, took these issues more seriously than Charles I. His efforts to rule
as he thought a king should rule led inadvertently to civil war and revolution
in the 1640s. Almost no one thought in terms of revolution in the 1640s,
but the proposals put forth as defenses of the rights of Parliament led gradually
to a significant shift in the institutional balance of power.

Religion played a major role in the British Revolution. In part, the
opposition to the Crown began to form because of royal support for religious
policies that established a relatively intolerant Anglican Church that too closely
resembled the Catholic Church. For those who considered themselves Puritans,
the religious issue was paramount. For others, it might simply be an example
of the king interfering in matters over which he had no jurisdiction. For many
supporters of Charles, of course, religious policies and institutions were also
important factors. And for a small number, religious beliefs led to radical
political, social, and economic ideas.

Origins of the British Revolution

While the politics of the 1620s and 1630s did not lead inexorably to rebellion and revolution in the 1640s, certain events did help create a situation that could easily become revolutionary. The policies followed by Charles I and his advisors in the 1620s, particularly in the arena of foreign affairs, produced some tension and opposition. The Petition of Rights (1628), based on various statutes and charters, sought to gain recognition for a few basic principles. Perhaps most important of these was the idea that taxes could not be levied without the consent of Parliament. Others included a reaffirmation of the right of *habeas corpus* (no one could be imprisoned without showing cause) and an insistence that soldiers could not be quartered in civilian homes or martial law declared in a time of peace. In return for his acceptance of the petition, Charles was granted subsidies. The next year, however, he dissolved Parliament and ruled in the 1630s without calling it back into session.

In the 1630s, royal policies connected with both religious affairs and fiscal matters continued to be unpopular. The ship money tax (a tax previously levied only on coastal areas to help pay for defense) in 1638 proved to be especially unpopular. The Anglican Church seemed headed toward "popery." Puritans wanted to abolish the office of bishop and end the use of the Book of Common Prayer. Presbyterians and other groups had their own ideas about how to organize the church. Religious policy spilled over easily into political questions. The idea that the Anglican Church was headed back toward Catholicism readily fed fears of papal plots to overthrown the English system of government.

It is not possible to sort the growing opposition to the Crown into neat categories. The old idea of an increasing gap between court and country is somewhat helpful, but supporters of the Crown could be found throughout England and in all levels of society. Important social, economic, and cultural changes were taking place. In particular, the growth of a commercial economy brought with it an increase in prices. Neither the rise to prominence of new social groups nor the decline of older groups, however, provides a key to the unfolding of events. At this time, no one was thinking in terms of revolution or even rebellion. There was mainly a growing dissatisfaction with royal policies, for which Charles unfortunately took responsibility.

The Scottish Rebellion in 1639 brought matters to a head. Primarily a rebellion against royal enforcement of Anglican religious practices, in particular the attempt to impose the Book of Common Prayer on the Presbyterians of Scotland, it created a political and fiscal crisis that required Charles to call a meeting of Parliament in 1640.

The "Short Parliament," which met for only three weeks, failed to vote funds for the war with Scotland. Charles then called what became the "Long Parliament." The immediate goal of the parliamentarians was the end of measures associated with eleven years of non-parliamentary rule and the removal from office of those responsible for these measures. A Triennial Act called for no more than three years to elapse between sessions of Parliament. Another act forbade the dissolution of Parliament without its consent. The ship money tax was declared illegal. Thomas Wentworth, Earl of Strafford, one of Charles's most important officials, was impeached for high treason and later executed. Archbishop William Laud, chief architect of Anglican religious policies, was imprisoned in the Tower of London.

This short period of reform might well have been the end of the political and fiscal crisis. One prominent view of the British Revolution holds that it was largely a matter of political mismanagement. In this view, more astute royal policies or a somewhat different royal personality might have appealed at this point to the large number of members of the House of Commons who had little interest in pressing issues to the point of civil war. Charles had to contend with issues raised by governing multiple kingdoms and those associated with religious division, problems his counterparts on the continent also contended with. However, revisionist scholars stress the importance of "the breakdown of a financial and political system in the face of inflation and the rising costs of war." This approach discounts the possibility of either social change or differences of political principles as important factors in the coming of civil war.

It does appear, nevertheless, that both social change and the construction of ideological positions helped to determine the outcome of the events from 1640 to 1642. While elites continued to take the lead in the events leading up to the civil war, there was a noticeable broadening of the political nation. Whether this broader political nation participated on the local or on the national scene, it redefined the parameters of political events. Religious policy was particularly important in this period and, as noted above, views on it easily spilled over into views about politics more generally. There were ideas about monarchical power based on notions of contract, law, and consent. If the "opposition" to the Crown largely preferred to find common ground with the monarchy, it nonetheless held a position it would not compromise.

New groups entered politics in 1641 and 1642. They included merchants and artisans, people who were not members of the traditional elites. London became a revolutionary city. In May 1641 thousands of people in the streets of London pressured the House of Lords to convict the Earl of Strafford, the chief minister of Charles; they also played a role in Charles's decision to sacrifice him. In December that year, popular pressure was again used to remove the bishops from the House of Lords. While these demonstrations were not completely spontaneous, they reflected support for Parliament, distrust of Charles's advisors, and fear of popish conspiracy.

The opposition did not trust Charles and saw in his actions attempts to regain control. They worried about his control of the military. Parliament was seen as the best defense against an arbitrary exercise of power. The situation was compounded by an Irish rebellion against English rule. Again, the rebellion in Ireland fanned fears of a popish conspiracy against the English people.

The failed attempt by Charles early in 1642 to arrest five leaders of the opposition in the House of Commons probably made civil war inevitable. For its part, Parliament presented a statement of nineteen demands in June 1642 that included not only reform of church and government along lines that it set but also parliamentary control of the military and of appointments of royal ministers. Such proposals had the effect of vesting sovereignty in Parliament, a position that Charles could not possibly support.

On the eve of civil war, a broad-based political nation stood divided on religious and political questions. Distrustful of the Crown, it was not necessarily committed to abolishing the monarchy. The civil war that began in the summer of 1642 created fertile ground for a polarization of opinions and for increasingly radical positions.

Civil war

By August 1642 opposing sides had formed, each claiming the same cause: they were the defenders of the true English political system and the Protestant religion. The two factions were also somewhat similar in social composition, and aristocratic elites furnished the leadership of each as well. While the king drew his strongest support from the House of Lords, a sizeable minority from the Commons also joined his cause. Anglicans and Catholics also tended to support the Crown. Geographically, the Crown's strength lay in the north and west.

The parliamentary group naturally drew much of its strength from members of the Commons. It also drew on the merchant and artisan classes in London, Norwich, Hull, Plymouth, and Gloucester. Geographically, its support came from the southeastern counties. In religious terms, it appealed to those who considered themselves Puritans and those from the more radical sects.

The early part of the civil war was indecisive, although one important development was the rapid rise to prominence of Oliver Cromwell, a member of the Long Parliament, as a military leader. The parliamentarians accepted the Solemn League and Covenant with the Presbyterian Scots in which they agreed not to establish a centralized national church. The influence of the Independents and the sectaries increased in the army, creating a widening gap between the army and Parliament.

In 1644 and 1645 the royal cause met defeat first at Marston Moor (1644), and then at Naseby (1645). Between these major battles, the parliamentary army was reorganized as the New Model Army with Cromwell as the main figure, although not the commander in chief. The first part of the civil war ended in 1646. The Scots delivered Charles to Parliament the following year.

In the meantime, differences of opinion between Parliament and the army developed. The army resisted attempts by Parliament to disband it. Soldiers worried not only about pay but also about the religious and political settlement proposed by Parliament. The Putney debates in 1647 showed the influence of the Levellers, a radical group interested in popular sovereignty and social equality. This represented a move away from doctrines that looked largely to the past and toward revolutionary change and universal ideas. Other groups, the Diggers, for example, with their ideas about collective ownership of property, were even more radical than the Levellers.

Charles, who had been captured by the army from the parliamentary party, refused to agree to the army council's peace terms (the Heads of the Proposals). He succeeded in escaping in November 1647 and, after negotiations with both Parliament and the Scots, allied with the Scots and began the second part of the civil war in 1648. The royalist cause was quickly crushed. In December 1648, the army removed its opponents in Parliament (Pride's Purge), reducing the Long Parliament to the Rump Parliament. This remnant erected a high court of justice, which tried the king for treason. Sentenced to death, Charles was beheaded on 30 January 1649.

The British Revolution of 1649?

The execution of the king opened a decade of experimentation. What should be put in place of a failed monarchy? Beyond abolishing the monarchy, had the English succeeded in carrying out a true revolution? Part of the answer may lie in the relationship between war and revolution. The French Revolution led to war and civil war. The problems experienced in preserving the revolution and simultaneously fighting a war and a civil war led increasingly desperate revolutionary leaders to corresponding radical measures. The French in the 1790s and also under Napoleon exported the revolutionary ideology and institutions throughout much of Europe. Civil war in England pushed the political process past several points at which moderates might have liked to stop, but not to the point of a coherent revolution in politics. England experienced war in the 1650s, but in the British Isles it was mainly a war of conquest in which Cromwell's army re-conquered Scotland and subdued Ireland. The brutality of subjection of Ireland, "the curse of Cromwell," left a legacy of bitterness that has yet to be overcome. Abroad, the British engaged in a naval war with the Dutch between 1652 and 1654. War and increases in property taxes and customs duties led to a crisis in 1653. Parliament considered disbanding the army, but Cromwell acted first, ending the Rump Parliament and declaring himself Lord Protector.

Essentially, Cromwell created a dictatorship in the 1650s, an ad hoc and personal solution that provided only a limited revolution and blocked, temporarily as it turned out, any chance of restoration. Seeing himself as the agent of God, Cromwell banned newspapers and used spies to keep track of possible dissent. While he allowed religious freedom in general terms, Catholics were not allowed to worship in public, nor could Anglicans use the Book of Common Prayer. His firm leadership kept this arrangement in place in the 1650s, although it could not completely stop the subversive activities of songwriters and pamphleteers. England in the 1650s did not undergo anything similar to the Terror in France in 1793–1794 (although it may be argued that the situation in Ireland was far worse). Cromwell's death in 1658 undid the arrangement, leading to political chaos and fear of renewed civil war. The Parliament elected in 1660 moved quickly to invite Charles II, son of the executed king, to return to the throne in 1660.

The abolition of the monarchy and the House of Lords was indeed enough to constitute a political revolution. For a few years, the parliamentary representatives of the people theoretically governed England. Radicals were dissatisfied with Parliament. The army itself was critical. In 1653 Cromwell assumed personal power. Nonetheless, the ideas and positions of the 1640s and even earlier could not be ignored, even if they could be temporarily set aside. Perhaps even more fundamental, politics came to be seen in a different light than had been the case earlier in England and than was the case at the time across the Channel. Both Hobbes and Locke emphasized the human element in politics. It was not something based on divine laws but rather created by men agreeing to a contract.

In religious matters, too, much had changed. A revived and powerful Anglican Church appeared with the restoration of the monarchy, but it was not able to suppress the Presbyterians and the more radical dissenters. Significant Protestant minorities continued to exist. They eventually won religious toleration, but continued to endure civil and political disabilities. The split between church and chapel played a significant role in English culture, education, and politics for more than two centuries after the British Revolution.

There was little that could be termed a social revolution. The Diggers, for example, were a tiny group of radicals. Some royalists lost property, but many avoided significant penalties. It was clearly not a bourgeois revolution. No class-conscious capitalist class emerged victorious over the feudal nobility. There was greater interest in commercial agriculture and in commerce more generally. Government began to be seen as having a positive role in such areas as colonial expansion rather than as a source of interference in economic matters. Perhaps paradoxically, the events of the revolution led to a stronger state but also one that existed within the context of a more individualized and commercialized society.

In terms of geography, the revolution established the centrality of England in British affairs and laid the basis for the creation of Great Britain. It emphasized as well the importance of London. Finally, the conquest of Ireland in the 1650s led to a social and economic transformation in that country with significant, long-lasting political implications.

The British Revolution was, to a very large extent, based on the defense of the historic political rights of the country. These appeals to the past nonetheless led to new departures. The idealized past became the basis for a fundamentally different system of government, although one certainly akin to the system that prevailed when Charles I ruled. The question might be raised, however, whether the events of the 1640s would be seen as revolutionary on their own and without the events of 1688 and 1689, forty years later. The short answer is most likely not. The Revolution of 1688 might easily have had a different outcome. That it continued and in a sense confirmed the British Revolution of the mid-century was not foreordained. Without the Revolution of 1688, the mid-century revolution would clearly have been seen as a failure, an interruption of political continuity.

The Revolution of 1688

Did Charles II and James II aspire to establish absolutism in England? Some evidence from events in the 1680s indicates a drift in that direction. Historians point to the relatively large army James organized in response to Monmouth's rebellion. Various important towns were effectively under martial law during his reign. James also worked to bring the judiciary under his control, appointing judges exclusively at the pleasure of the Crown. This allowed him to purge the bench when necessary in order to appoint judges who would do his bidding.

Charles II had also strengthened the royal prerogative. He had been challenged by Parliament, particularly with the Test Act of 1673 that required all government officials to profess allegiance to the Church of England, and again in 1678 when Parliament explicitly denied the throne to a Roman Catholic. In the latter case, Charles refused to allow the action to become law. He worked actively against attempts made by Parliament to exclude his brother from succession by favoring the Tories against the Whigs. Tories supported a strong, hereditary monarchy while Whigs favored parliamentary supremacy. Many feared that the Exclusion crisis might lead to another civil war and that the Whigs favored a republic.

James, too, might have continued to strengthen the royal prerogative, but only if this were done in the service of the Tories and the Church of England. Religion was the stumbling block. Using his power to advance the interests of Roman Catholics led to resistance. A contemporary noted that it was the mixture of "popery and arbitrary power" that most of his subjects would not accept. Although 1688 is often seen as a Whig revolution, many of its supporters would have been the king's allies except for the issue of religion.

Having lost the support of many Anglicans, some of them Tories, James attempted in 1687 to ally with Whigs and Dissenters. While many were dubious, others were prepared to cooperate. Many of those willing to cooperate came from a level below that of the political elite. In many respects, then, the Revolution of 1688 was a conservative movement to restore the traditional rulers in the provinces to power. Those who sought to work with the king looked to him as the best chance to gain toleration. With the help of the king, they would pack Parliament, which would serve their purpose, to obtain an

Act of Parliament establishing toleration by enacting the king's Declaration of Indulgence, and the Crown's purpose, to secure a Parliament that would do his bidding.

What chance James II may have had in alliance with the Whigs and Dissenters he lost by reversing his policies once he learned that William, the husband of his elder daughter Mary and the ruler of the Dutch Republic, was about to sail to England with troops. As W. A. Speck notes, James II, reversing himself in an attempt to reassure his old allies, the Anglican Tories, succeeded only "in revealing his total unreliability" ("1688: A Political Revolution," in David Parker, ed., *Revolution and Revolutionary Tradition in the West, 1560–1991*, London and New York: Routledge, p. 62).

James II created a difficult situation for himself, but only in the larger context of European politics was this situation fatal. William of Orange issued a declaration in September 1688 that emphasized problems created by violations of "the law, liberties [privileges] and customs," in particular those affecting religion. However, his main interest was to prevent England from aligning itself with Louis XIV's France. Louis could have easily prevented the invasion, but he shifted his troops away from a location near the borders of the Dutch Republic to a location about two hundred miles away. The navy, which also could have prevented the invasion, was deployed to the Mediterranean to put pressure on the papacy.

Some call attention to the fact that William's troops were probably not sufficient to defeat James. If this analysis is correct, James may have missed an opportunity to confront and defeat William. Even if James had been defeated, he still might have won the day by confronting William. One possibility is that he distrusted his own high command. Given that Lord Churchill, the future Duke of Marlborough, sided with William, this was a justifiable suspicion.

In any case, in December 1688 William asked James to leave London and he did; a few days later he fled to France. On Christmas Eve, the peers, meeting in the House of Lords, asked William to call a Convention and to govern the country in the meantime. Effectively, William became the king, but this did not become official until he accepted the offer of the Crown on 13 February 1689.

In 1685 James had not yet had time to alienate his subjects and they backed him against Monmouth's rebellion. By 1688, many of his supporters were no longer ready to accept his unconditional restoration. James, for his part, would not agree to conditions.

If there was a consensus that William must replace James, only a few actively participated in the revolutionary events. Those elected to the Convention generally condemned what they saw as James's arbitrary actions and wanted to ensure that monarchs would not be able to act in such a way in the future. Those who had cooperated with the king earlier found their cooperation was held against them.

At the Convention, participants divided on what to do. A few believed James still held the throne by divine right and should be called back to resume it. Another small group favored a republic. The majority recognized the constitutional impasse and chose to accept the idea of limited monarchy over either absolute monarchy or republic. The Declaration of Rights declared thirteen measures undertaken by James to be illegal and asserted parliamentary limitations on a monarch's freedom of action. The changes in the Coronation Oath reflected this position. James swore to "grant and keep" the law that had been "granted by the kings of England." William and Mary swore "to govern the people . . . according to the statutes in parliament agreed on. . . ."

Various solutions, among them a regency or Mary as queen, were suggested, but William's threat to leave the country with his army if he were not given the Crown ended the discussion. He and his wife became joint rulers. Parliament assured that the monarchy was limited by keeping them financially dependent.

Those who carried out the Revolution of 1688 were reluctant revolutionaries, as W. A. Speck terms them in his book on 1688, *Reluctant Revolutionaries*. In one sense they continued and confirmed the main lines of the British Revolution of the mid-century, with the emphasis on the place of Parliament in the English system of government. In another, they reacted to what the British Revolution had done, working to preserve the House of Lords as a locus of political power and the Anglican Church as the established church, and working to prevent pressures from below from pushing the revolution further than they wanted it to go. Paradoxically, they were also reacting to a threat from above, the attempts by James II to replace limited monarchy with absolute monarchy, and especially his efforts to gain equal status for his fellow Catholics. The latter was seen as a deliberate effort to return the established church to Rome. Although Tories and Whigs temporarily allied to prevent James from undermining the ancient constitution, the Whigs fared better in the aftermath of the revolution because they were ready to accept it and its consequences.

Conclusion

By the end of the eighteenth century, certainly after the twin traumas of the American Revolution and the French Revolution, the British were prone to forget their own revolutionary experiences. The nineteenth century, with its repeated spectacle of revolution in France and the widespread revolutionary movement of 1848, only reinforced this historical amnesia. The Wilkes affair in the 1760s, which raised issues of parliamentary corruption and resulted in calls for reform, was echoed in the Great Reform of 1832. In both cases, the state was strong enough to resist the pressures of the masses. In the latter case, the state, perhaps under the influence of the French Revolution of 1830 as well as massive demonstrations in Britain, passed reforms that removed many of the chief complaints about the practices of British politics at the time.

However close to a renewal of revolution or distant from it, the main point is that even Britain, which prided itself on political stability, might have resorted again to revolutionary means of politics.

The product of the revolutionary events of the seventeenth century, a limited monarchy based on constitutional documents and statements of rights, had a powerful impact in the eighteenth century. *Philosophes* commented favorably on the representative nature of the English political system and the opportunities for widespread participation in political affairs, especially on the local level. Voltaire, in particular, contrasted England with France, both in terms of its superior political system and its more open society. The British colonies in North America fought in the American Revolution to establish a political system that although it lacked a king and was far more democratic, in many other respects resembled the British political system. Some commentators view the American Revolution as little more than the ratification of a system derived in large part from the British. That this was not the end of the American Revolution, with its bloody revival in the American Civil War, and a violent echo in the Civil Rights Movement in the 1950s and 1960s, is not a story that can be rehearsed here. The point is that the English revolutionary events of the seventeenth century had repercussions beyond that century and that country. The British Revolution was not simply the first modern revolution, but it also helped in tangible ways to lay the foundations for the two major revolutions that formed the prevailing ideas about the means and goals of revolution down to the Russian Revolution of 1917. It is difficult to imagine the American Revolution taking place at all without the British Revolution coming before it. The French Revolution had other sources in addition to the British Revolution, but nonetheless owed much to that event.

What sets the British Revolution apart from the French Revolution is the emphasis in the former on preservation or conservation. The product of events in seventeenth-century England was a limited monarchy, one that evolved over the next two centuries into a constitutional monarchy, in many respects something quite different from what had existed before the British Revolution. It was the sense of only trying to retain something hallowed by custom and tradition and the reluctance to try anything that seemed too innovative that kept the British Revolution largely a study in moderation. Participants were revolutionaries, but they were cautious and moderate in the ways in which they went about conducting the revolution. To be sure, there were those in the British Revolution who wished to go much further, in both politics and in social matters, but those in power had little trouble curtailing their influence. In the French Revolution, while many would have been satisfied with a constitutional monarchy, one could not be put together satisfactorily. This presented an opening to those who hoped to establish a new and supposedly far superior political system. The pressure of war and civil war in France led participants to the practice of terror and an extreme kind of social engineering.

The history of revolution, at least from the late eighteenth century, has featured an oscillation between limited, largely pragmatic goals and the more utopian and comprehensives efforts. Revolutions generally have featured both tendencies. Their outcomes have depended on which tendency gained the upper hand. The British Revolution in the mid-century failed to find a moderate solution. Instead, it turned into a repressive dictatorship. More important, however, it left a legacy the Revolution of 1688 could refer back to and use for its own ends. That legacy, as modified by the Revolution of 1688, then furnished the basis for a long period of evolutionary development.

Further reading

Mid-century

Hughes, Ann (1998) *The Causes of the English Civil War*, second edition. New York: St. Martin's.

Kishlansky, Mark (1996) *A Monarchy Transformed: Britain 1603–1714*. London: Penguin.

Russell, Conrad (1990) *Unrevolutionary England 1603–1642*. London: Hambledon Press.

Underdown, David (1996) *A Freeborn People: Politics and the Nation in Seventeenth-Century England*. Oxford: Clarendon Press.

Woolrych, Austin (2003) *Britain in Revolution, 1625–1660*. New York and Oxford: Oxford University Press.

1688

Israel, Jonathan (1991) *The Anglo-Dutch Moment: Essays on the Revolution of 1688 and Its World Impact*. Cambridge and New York: Cambridge University Press.

Jones, J. R. (editor) (1992) *Liberty Secured? Britain Before and After 1688*. Stanford, CA: Stanford University Press.

Speck, W. A. (1988) *Reluctant Revolutionaries: Englishmen and the Revolution of 1688*. Oxford and New York: Oxford University Press.

Chapter 3

The Mexican Revolution

The Mexican Revolution was the first great political and social revolution of the twentieth century. It was also one of a cluster of revolutions occurring at about the same time in Russia, China, the Ottoman Empire, and Iran (then called Persia). These revolutions, particularly those in Russia and China, had an enormous impact on the history of the twentieth century.

The Mexican Revolution in its revolutionary decade, 1910–1920, features bloodshed, betrayal, and cruelty, as well as class struggle, intervention by the United States, and a colorful assembly of larger-than-life revolutionaries. Overall, it illustrates those characteristics of revolution discussed in the previous chapter. Of primary importance, the revolution was a product of Mexican history, one way of responding to the political situation created by the regime of Porfirio Díaz. And it shaped the way politics were done for the remainder of the twentieth century.

In the twenty years that followed the chaos and dislocation of the revolutionary decade, those Mexicans who had gained power in the revolution used that power, sometimes with great thoughtfulness, at other times more with simple cunning, to rebuild and reshape their country. It was a contentious process, often punctuated by violence, especially in the 1920s. Both idealism and opportunism flourished. Idealism seemingly triumphed in the 1930s, when revolutionary momentum on various levels found a leadership, personified in Lázaro Cárdenas, sympathetic to its goals. After 1940, however, the revolution lost its way. Opportunists, like the ones described by Carlos Fuentes in his brilliant novel, *The Death of Artemio Cruz*, rose to the top and essentially murdered the revolution. They embalmed the corpse of the revolution and put it on display. It endured for the remainder of the century, mostly as form and rhetoric. No one, even as the system began to unravel in the 1980s, found a way to move beyond the sterile politics and social injustice that characterized Mexican life in the late twentieth century.

The revolutionary decade (1910–1920)

The revolutionary decade began with the problems experienced by the regime of Porfirio Díaz. Long-lived (1876–1910) and successful for most of its existence, the Díaz regime emphasized economic growth and a strong central government. It grew, however, increasingly dependent on foreign investment and the global market.

While economic problems and the development of a Mexican nationalism lessened the popularity of the regime in the first decade of the twentieth century, it floundered initially on the issue of *continuismo*, i.e. the modification of constitutional arrangements to allow Díaz to continue in office. Liberals in Mexico spent the first decade of the twentieth century calling for free elections and a constitution that worked. Organized in the Partido Liberal Mexicano (PLM) in 1906, they worked in Mexico and in exile in the United States to end the Díaz regime. Franciso Madero, a member of the Coahuila provincial elite, landowner, industrialist, and banker, who was often called "The Apostle of Democracy," challenged *continuismo* with a book entitled *The Presidential Succession of 1910* (1908). He later campaigned against Díaz in 1910. To the extent that ideology helped to bring about the revolution, the ideology that initially influenced the Mexican Revolution was an older liberal one that called for constitutions, representative bodies, and free elections.

Although the constitutional challenge was important, there were other factors behind the challenge to the regime. The regime had long been concerned with economic growth and with its role in the emerging world economy. The very success of the regime's policies also created two problems. The first was the expansion of foreign investment. Foreigners held approximately one-third of the land in Mexico at the turn of the century. They dominated industry and held important stakes in mining and timber. American holdings in both agriculture and industry were particularly large. Secondly, in the last few years of the Díaz regime, developments in the world economy damaged important sectors of the Mexican economy, especially agriculture, mining, timber, and textiles. Unemployment was high in industry and mining. Small businessmen also suffered from the economic downturn. Bad harvests in 1908 and 1909 led to famine and food riots.

Economic contraction, in turn, influenced two other aspects of the revolution. One was nationalism, in particular, the belief that foreigners had undue influence on Mexican politics. The second was the vulnerability of regional elites (Coahuila and Sonora in particular), who found their economic interests jeopardized by the policies of a regime on which they had little or no influence.

In the spring of 1910 the Anti-Re-electionist Party nominated Madero as a candidate for president. Arrested by Díaz, he spent Election Day in prison in San Luis Potosi. Diaz was, not surprisingly, re-elected. In September, Díaz celebrated his eightieth birthday and the centennial of Mexican independence. The following month, Madero, released on bail, escaped to San Antonio, Texas. There he issued the first of the many plans in the revolution, the Plan of San Luis Potosi. Primarily a political document, it promised democracy and federalism but also mentioned the right of workers to bargain collectively and agrarian reform.

The combination of a regime experiencing heavy criticism and open challenge and the disintegration of the social consensus of the elites opened the floodgates to a torrent of ideas, aspirations, and schemes. Centers of revolution developed in Chihuahua under Pascual Orozco, Jr. and in Morelos under Emiliano Zapata. Other ideologies, in particular anarcho-syndicalism, a radical movement emphasizing the power and influence of trade unions, and a kind of agrarian populism among the peasants, gained prominence.

Over the next few years, the revolution existed essentially on two levels. The first level involved the elites. They emphasized politics, nationalism, and the revival of a stagnant economy. They gathered support from the middle and lower middle classes, including businessmen, merchants, the *intelligentsia*, bureaucrats, and local officials. Aware of the needs of the working class and the peasantry, they were, however, not willing to venture far in the direction of social reform. Early on, the most prominent representative of this group was Madero.

The second level included mostly workers and peasants, those most directly affected by the economic problems associated with the Díaz regime. While clearly interested in what political arrangements the revolution might produce, they emphasized social and economic issues. In part, they stressed the defense of the traditional. This could be seen especially in the followers of Zapata. They wished to regain their communal lands from those, Mexicans and foreigners alike, who had used the legal system to gain ownership, and to re-establish largely autonomous municipalities. They did not, however, simply wish to turn the clock back. They recognized, for example, the importance of collective bargaining rights for the working class.

Luis Cervantes, the representative of the *intelligentsia* in Mariano Azuela's novel *The Underdogs* (*Los de abajo*), waxes eloquent on the motives of the revolutionaries:

> It is not true you [Demetrio Macias, the protagonist of *The Underdogs*] took up arms simply because of Señor Monico. You are under arms to protest against the evils of all the *caciques* [political bosses] who are overrunning the whole nation. We are the elements of a social movement which will not rest until it has enlarged the destinies of our motherland. We are the tools Destiny makes use of to reclaim the sacred rights of the people. We are not fighting to dethrone a miserable murderer, we are fighting against tyranny itself.

The reality, of course, is that motives were mixed. Some saw the revolution as a grand struggle for justice in the face of tyranny. Many, perhaps most, had more concrete aims.

Madero gained broad support in 1911 and defeated Díaz. In the fall he took office as president. Although aware of the need for land reform, his initial measures seemed designed more for speculators than for *campesinos*. In less than a month after Madero took office, he faced the opposition of Zapata. Zapata was a trainer of horses and a stable master. Elected to local office in 1909 in the village of Anenecuilco, Morelos, he was deeply sympathetic to the problems of the peasants. In his own plan, the Plan of Ayala (November 1911), Zapata advanced a radical agenda for land reform. He called for land redistribution in the form of communes and cooperatives and also for the return of municipal autonomy. He also advocated democracy and collective bargaining rights for the working class.

Pascual Orozco, who had combined cowboys, miners, lumberjacks, Indians, and farmers in Chihuahua into a force that was originally Maderista, emerged as the major opponent of Madero. He, too, issued a radical plan of social reform, the Plan Orozquista (March 1912). Zapata and Orozco, although unable to coordinate their individual efforts effectively, nonetheless were a formidable opposition to Madero by 1913. In the meantime, Madero failed to win support from the industrial workers who formed the Casa del Obrero Mundial, a workers' council in Mexico City in 1912.

The greatest danger to Madero, however, came from reactionaries, opportunists, and foreigners. Felix Díaz, a nephew of the former dictator, had already rebelled once against Madero and had been defeated and arrested. Gaining release from prison, he rebelled again in February 1913. This rebellion also failed and Felix Díaz found himself besieged in an old fortress in Mexico City. The commander of the federal troops, Victoriano Huerta, came to an agreement with Díaz. He also concluded the Pacto de la Embajada with the American ambassador, Henry Lane Wilson. The main idea of the agreement with the American ambassador was to remove Madero from power in favor of Felix Díaz. Huerta, however, managed to make himself president. In the process he had President Madero and José María Pino Suarez, his vice-president, murdered.

Huerta's cynical opportunism led to a civil war that engulfed large portions of Mexico from 1913 to 1917. Huerta gained the backing of Orozco, but he was opposed by many of the elites. The most important of these, Governor Venustiano Carranza of Coahuila, detested Huerta's regime and issued his own plan in response to it, the Plan of Guadalupe (1913), a document almost exclusively concerned with politics. Zapata, of course, still looking for support for land reform, opposed Huerta even more strongly than he had Madero. Pancho Villa, who had fought in 1910–1911 under Orozco, emerged as an important new opponent in Chihuahua, where he gathered cowboys, sharecroppers, miners, and lumberjacks into a first-class fighting unit, the Division del Norte, the most powerful rebel force in the revolution. Where Zapata was the leader of a community, Villa seemed more the man on horseback (he was a superb horseman). Brave, charismatic, dedicated to his men, and an excellent organizer and manager, he was not all bravado, however. He believed in the redistribution of income from the rich to the poor and noted the importance of education. Most of all, he seemed interested in a return to the autonomy enjoyed by what had been frontier communities in Chihuahua. In this respect, both he and Zapata wanted to return to a world that governed itself with minimal interference from Mexico City. Like Zapata, too, he was a regionalist, uncomfortable on the national stage.

In the chaos of warring factions, American intervention once again forced the revolution in a particular direction. In April 1914 the US Navy launched an attack on the Mexican port of Veracruz. After a naval bombardment, the US Army secured and occupied the city. In November 1914 the American government decided to back Carranza's Constitutionalist army as the faction most likely to respect American interests in Mexico. It used its position in Veracruz to equip Carranza's army. The army received some 12,000 rifles and carbines, over three million rounds of ammunition, machine guns, barbed wire, cars, trucks, and artillery. These supplies were crucial in the eventual Constitutionalist defeat of Villa's forces.

Between the American occupation of Veracruz and the resupply of Carranza's troops, Villa had repeatedly defeated Huerta's forces, forcing Huerta to give up the presidency and flee the country. In the summer of 1914, even though Huerta had left the revolutionary stage, Carranza was still no match for Villa and his ally Zapata, neither in terms of military strength nor political following.

Alvaro Obregón Salido, who had not participated in the Maderista revolt of 1910–1911, was on the fringes of the elites socially. He soon, however, became the indispensable man for Carranza and the Constitutionalists. Obregón not only wanted to liberalize politics, he also presented an extensive social agenda that included agrarian and industrial reform. He could step outside the elite view of the world and understand the needs of other social groups in Mexico. He eventually became the most important figure in the first, most violent phase of the revolution.

Obregón made two significant contributions to the Constitutionalist position in 1914. First, he courted the working class, organized in the Casa del Obrero Mundial, and the urban intellectuals. The workers provided important support for the army. When Carranza's stance on land reform, which stressed the importance of observing property rights, was widely denounced by Villista and Zapatista leaders, Obregón arranged a meeting between the two sides at Aguascalientes in October.

The convention at Aguascalientes brought the followers of Villa and Zapata closer together and made clear their differences with Carranza. It also made plain the radical nature of their ideas, effectively pitting them against Carranza and Obregón. Stunned American observers made the fateful decision to support Carranza and Obregón.

At the end of the year, Villa and Zapata met for the first time at Xochimilco. As an American agent (quoted in John Womack's fine biography of Zapata) described the scene, Villa was "tall, robust, weighing about 180 pounds . . . wearing an English [pith] helmet, a heavy brown sweater, khaki trousers, leggings and heavy riding shoes." Zapata was much shorter than Villa, "weighing probably 130 pounds . . . [and wearing] a short black coat, a large light blue silk neckerchief, pronounced lavender shirt . . . [and] a pair of black, tight-fitting Mexican trousers with silver buttons down the outside seam of each leg." The two chiefs, at first at a loss for words, eventually found common ground in their dislike of Carranza. They were unable, however, to effectively coordinate their armies. While the nation saw them as a united force, they continued to fight largely separate campaigns, which weakened each of their positions greatly.

In 1915 Obregón's reorganized and well-equipped armies defeated Villa's forces in a series of battles from April to June. Obregón applied the lessons the Great War was teaching the world and used barbed wire and carefully placed machine guns to good effect. He also had the use of modern artillery provided by the Americans.

While Obregón defeated Villa, Zapata continued to hold the south and the center of Mexico. At the same time, working-class radicalism, centered on the Casa del Obrero Mundial, formed a growing threat to the Constitutionalist movement. A strike in May 1916 resulted in victory for the Casa. When few of the promises made in May were kept, a renewed strike in July found the government better prepared. It used the army to break the power of the anarcho-syndicalist unions.

Villa, despite defeat by Obregon, continued to be troublesome. His raid on Columbus, New Mexico, early in 1916, resulted in the "Punitive Expedition" led by General John J. Pershing. Villa became an almost legendary figure, but could not translate this into effective political power.

While the fighting continued, the Constitutionalists staged a meeting in 1916 at Queretaro. This was a very different affair from the meeting two years prior at Aguascalientes. Fewer military leaders were present. Instead there were more people with university educations and professional backgrounds. Out of the meeting came the Constitution of 1917, the most important document in twentieth-century Mexican history.

The Constitution of 1917 created a series of reforms that would lay the foundation for a new Mexican government. It called for separation of church and state, the right to education through public schools, the regulation of working conditions, and the right of workers to form unions and to strike. It also empowered the government to redistribute land. This meant not simply restoring land illegally seized from the peasantry. It also made possible the expropriation of land that was not serving a useful purpose. Finally, it also asserted that the nation owned the subsoil resources. Nearly every group in the Mexican Revolution found something in the Constitution it had been fighting for. The Constitution, a clear repudiation of laissez-faire liberalism, owed much to the plans, especially the Plan Orozquista and the Plan de Ayala. It was, however, a document of reform, not of revolution.

The costs of the revolution were enormous. In a nation with a population of roughly 15 million, between 1.5 and 2 million died. Many of the leaders of the revolution were assassinated. The first was Emiliano Zapata in April 1919. He became a martyr. Carranza was held responsible for Zapata's death and lost a great deal of popularity. The following year Carranza attempted to handpick his successor. To many, workers, peasants, and even the Americans, this could only mean a continuation of a regime that seemed unable to address the basic problems of the country. His former lieutenant, Obregón, who had resigned after the assassination of Zapata, led a march on Mexico City that deposed the isolated Carranza. Carranza was assassinated later that year.

The Mexican Revolution, while occurring at the same time as the Great War and revolutions all around the world, had followed and continued to follow its own path. It had broadened the practice of politics and given voice not only to provincial and local elites but also to the urban middle classes and the workers. It had done the least for the majority of the population, the peasants. But even for them it had made promises and created a constitutional basis for action on those promises. The Constitution of 1917 had set an agenda that was basically democratic and progressive. The revolutionaries had seized and reconstituted power. It now remained to be seen how effectively they would use it.

Using power (1920–1940)

Reconstruction was the most important task of the 1920s. This was, however, no easy task given the lack of institutions and governmental processes, the absence of consensus as to how to proceed, and the continuing tendency to use violence to resolve differences of opinion. The Constitution of 1917 provided a basic plan for reconstruction, but in 1920 it offered little more than promises. To what extent could the government turn those promises into realities?

Obregón brought with him from Sonora people with administrative experience and political skills. He, Adolfo de la Huerta, and Plutarco Elías Calles counted themselves as hardheaded realists. They were eager to repeat on a national level what they had been able to accomplish in Sonora.

The new government emphasized reconciliation. It negotiated the retirement of Pancho Villa in 1920 and ended the conflict with the Zapatistas and other regional rebels. It also welcomed the return of former opponents of Carranza to political life. Members of the government saw themselves as successors to Madero, as the true representatives of the Mexican Revolution. The new slogan was "The Revolution transformed into government" ("*La Revolucion hecha gobierno*").

Obregón reached out as well to different interest groups. He had already formed an alliance with the Regional Confederation of Mexican Workers (CROM), the most important organization for workers for most of the 1920s. He also sponsored land redistribution in areas where peasant unrest was most pronounced.

Although Obregón was acknowledged as the undisputed *caudillo* or political boss in Mexico, he had to contend with regional leaders and with the large revolutionary army. Mass politics served as a counterweight to the ambitious politicians and generals.

As the end of his term neared, Obregón worked to organize a peaceful transition. Relations with the United States had improved, leading to formal recognition of the Mexican government in 1923. Earlier, in the spring, Villa's assassination removed any possibility he might take advantage of the transition period. Calles announced as his candidacy for the presidency. The beneficiary of Obregón's support, Calles won the election.

A massive rebellion nonetheless broke out in December 1923. The government, backed by organized labor and the peasants, put down the rebellion by March the following year. A by-product of the failed rebellion was a smaller, less dangerous military.

President Calles had a reputation of being more radical and more nationalistic than Obregón. During his term in office, he continued Obregón's policies, maintaining a good relationship with labor, extending land redistribution, expanding the railroad system, and building rural schools. Overall, however, presidential power grew at the expense of increasingly dependent states.

In the course of the 1920s, the United States came to view Mexico with suspicion. Influenced by the emergence of Soviet Russia, some in Washington considered the Calles government a Bolshevik government and talked about "Soviet Mexico." Internally, the passage of anticlerical legislation in 1926 led to the Cristero Rebellion in west-central Mexico. It began with the declaration of a strike by the Roman Catholic Church on July 31, 1926. For three years, priests did not celebrate mass, baptize babies, or give the dying the last rites. Between 1927 and 1929, bands of Cristeros attacked the government under the slogan of "Viva Christ the King!" ("*Viva Cristo Rey!*"). Tens of thousands of Mexicans died in a renewal of a civil war with a distinctive religious basis.

At the end of Calles' term, whether Obregón would return to office became the major political question. The Constitution had been amended in 1927 to permit one nonconsecutive re-election, and in 1928 the presidential term extended to six years. Obregón ran for office and won re-election in July 1928.

Obregón survived two assassination attempts but he did not survive the third. Calles, in an attempt to head off chaos, resisted the idea of re-election and instead handed the presidency to a candidate acceptable to both his supporters and those of Obregón. In all, there were three presidents between 1928 and 1934, a period known as the *Maximato*. Calles, the most powerful man in the country despite his lack of office, became known as the *Jefe Maximo* (Supreme Chief).

Under the first of the three presidents, the government negotiated an end to the Cristero Rebellion and improved relations with the United States. In 1929 both the Callistas and the Obregónistas cooperated to form a federation of the state and regional revolutionary parties, the National Revolutionary Party (PNR). Within the PNR, a revitalized agrarian movement became increasingly influential. Calles could not counterbalance it with CROM, the labor movement, in that CROM was excluded from the PNR because of its opposition to Obregón's re-election.

In 1933 the agrarian forces established the National Peasant Confederation and called for the renewal of agrarian reform. Working within the PNR, they supported the nomination of Lazaro Cardenas as candidate for president in 1934. Calles did not oppose the will of the party he had created and agreed to the nomination of Cardenas. He likely endorsed him with the idea in mind he could use Cardenas, a friend and loyal supporter in the past, as he had used previous presidents.

Even though Cardenas's election was assured, he campaigned throughout Mexico. He apparently sought a popular mandate for a continuation of the revolution. Elected in July 1934, he took office the following December and began what essentially formed a second revolution, a period of rapid and radical change. In several ways, it resembled the Stalin Revolution in the Soviet Union, also in the 1930s. It featured a reorganization of agriculture, although one that had very different results from the Soviet effort. It solidified a political system that endured for the next few decades, again a very different system from that of the Soviet Union. Finally, it emphasized the creation of a Mexican identity and encouraged a feeling of national pride in Mexico, again superficially similar to Stalin's efforts to create the new Soviet man and woman and pride in the Soviet Union. Cardenas's efforts, however, while revolutionary, were far more moderate and involved relatively little violence. Still, Mexico at the end of the 1930s was quite different from what it had been at the beginning of the decade.

The initial problem the government faced was what to do with the *Jefe Maximo*. Calles expected to continue to manage political affairs from behind the scenes, but Cardenas worked in the first year to retire or replace army generals and state governors allied with Calles. He also accelerated land reform and tolerated the strike movement, gaining the support of agrarian and labor organizations. When Calles began to criticize government policy in 1935, Cardenas purged his cabinet of Calles's supporters. The Cardenistas took over the PNR, the Congress, and the governments of a number of states.

It took several additional months for the game to play out. Cardenas had Calles put on a plane for the United States in April 1936 and sent into what was in effect exile. Unlike so many of the other leaders of the Mexican Revolution, Calles was not assassinated. The *Maximato* ended peacefully.

The main thrust of Cardenas' policy concerned the welfare of the average Mexican. Two interconnected activities were necessary for his policy to work. One involved a reduction of the power of the *hacienda* or large estate. The other called for the construction of the *ejido*, communally owned land that could be worked either communally or by individuals.

In 1935 land grants quadrupled. The next year, with the end of the *Maximato*, even more dramatic actions took place. Cardenas expropriated many of the richest zones of commercial agriculture in the country and provided funding for tractors and other equipment through the National Ejidal Credit Bank. During his administration some fifty million acres were distributed to about 800,000 peasants. More than 11,000 *ejidos* were established. At the end of the decade, one of Cardenas's ideologues wrote: "We must always keep in mind that it is people and their happiness and not the production of wealth that matters." The governments that followed soon altered this radical perspective.

Cardenas also courted labor. The PNR's Six-Year Plan called for increased state intervention in the economy and Cardenas gave the labor movement free rein to strike, particularly against foreign firms. In 1936 a number of unions came together to create the Confederation of Mexican Workers (CTM). Vicente Lombardo Toledano, the major figure in the CTM, worked to gain CTM endorsement of the policies of the government. The confederation also participated with the PNR in electoral politics.

The alliance between government and labor led to the most dramatic event of the Cardenas government, the expropriation of the foreign-owned petroleum industry in March 1938. After a local federal arbitration board ruled in favor of an increase in wages and improved social benefits for workers, oil companies appealed to the Federal Conciliation and Arbitration Board. When it ruled in favor of the workers, the oil companies again balked and Cardenas acted. It was, in effect, a declaration of economic independence and was wildly popular in Mexico. It echoed one of the main themes of the Mexican Revolution and might justly be considered a high point of the second phase of the revolution.

In line with the social and economic changes, Cardenas also transformed Calles's party into a party based on the CTM and the newly created National Peasant Confederation (CNC). Other sectors of the new party included the military and a unit composed largely of state employees. The 1938 party convention accepted these changes and gave the party a new name: the Party of the Mexican Revolution (PRM).

Cardenas's government also instituted a cultural revolution. The cultural revolution in Mexico aimed primarily at the creation of a new Mexican national identity. This meant, first of all, fighting the influence of the Catholic Church. More positively, like the great social revolutions in Russia and later in China, revolutionaries in Mexico wanted to create new revolutionary men and women. They wanted to bring Mexicans from all regions and classes together in a process that might be termed "Mexicanization." The battleground for Mexicanization, the creation of a republican and secular outlook, was the school. One person in particular, José Vasconselos, made the cultural revolution of the 1930s possible through his educational reforms in the 1920s. He created a system of rural primary schools, which by 1936 included some 11,000 schools, 14,000 teachers, and more than 700,000 children. It was an impressive accomplishment although not nearly enough. Estimates were that twice as many rural schoolteachers were needed. This educational reform was reminiscent of educational efforts in the French Third Republic in the era before World War I. One official in the Ministry of Public Education (SEP) commented in 1926 that "Our little rural school stands for Mexico and represents Mexico in those far-off corners – so many of them that belong to Mexico but are not yet Mexico."

The cultural revolution accelerated in the 1930s. In particular, the Cardenista policy and ideology of *indigenismo* took root. *Indigenismo* opposed the older idea of civilizing the Indians. Rather, it called for the promotion of the social, economic, and spiritual emancipation of Indians while at the same time it preserved the best of native culture. Those in charge of the work of preservation often made unfounded assumptions about Indians and their heritage, which often produced representations of that heritage that were not authentic. Nonetheless, the intention was to improve the life of Mexico's Indians and to preserve their culture. Indian heritage received new prominence and acceptance.

Mexico's cultural revolution shocked some, while disappointing others by not going far enough. By the 1940s, however, it had created a somewhat different Mexico, one in which most young people had learned to read and write. The Mexico heavily influenced by France that many had criticized during the Porfiriato had been Mexicanized. Mexicans now saw themselves and their country differently. This was portrayed artistically in the stunning murals of José Clemente Orozco and Diego Rivera. While Orozco painted what the revolution had been, Rivera painted what it should have been. Both glorified Mexico, its people, customs, and history. In many ways, however, Mexico's cultural revolution, while bringing the country together, obscured the importance of the several regions into which Mexico was then still divided.

The "death" of the revolution

In the 1940 presidential race, the PRM faced a choice between a Cardenista candidate, the radical Francisco Mugica, and a more moderate figure, General Manuel Ávila Camacho, Cardenas's defense minister. Cardenas believed the PRM was "a revolutionary instrument" that would continue the revolution and did not try to influence the choice of the PRM's candidate. It chose Ávila Camacho.

Although Ávila Camacho promised "to consolidate the gains of the Cardenas regime," his government took Mexico in another direction. This could be seen plainly in the lack of attention paid to land reform and the *ejido*. Land redistribution slowed to a crawl during Ávila Camacho's time in office. Even more important, the government failed to make available to the *ejidos* the necessary financing and the other kinds of assistance farmers needed.

Not coincidentally, the Rockefeller Foundation and the Mexican Ministry of Agriculture established the Mexican Agricultural Project in 1943. Its work formed the basis for the "Green Revolution" of hybrid grains. The emphasis in Mexican agricultural affairs shifted from the *ejidos* to commercial agriculture and the private sector. The Cardenista project of a rural Mexico of prosperous *ejidos* remained uncompleted. It may have been a utopian approach in many respects, and its attempt at social engineering ran counter to the economic trends of the twentieth century.

The government under Ávila Camacho also emphasized industrialization. Taking advantage of the demand created by World War II, Mexican industry grew by an average of 10 percent a year between 1940 and 1945. Labor, in the form of the CTM, went along with the policy of industrialization. In the postwar period, the CTM was strengthened at the expense of the labor movement more generally in an effort to keep wages low and make foreign investment attractive.

Finally, Ávila Camacho changed Cardenas's "revolutionary instrument," the PRM, to offset the power of the labor and peasant sectors. In 1946 it was reconstituted as the Party of the Institutional Revolution (PRI) and the authority of the leadership strengthened.

The government and its supporters in the PRI established a vision of a modern Mexico reminiscent of the vision of the *cientificos*, the supporters of industrialization, foreign investment, and technological progress in the Porfirean era. Essentially, they brought the revolution to an end. It had served its purpose. Now industry, commerce, science, technology, foreign capital, all these were to be used to create a vibrant, urban, modern state and society.

In itself an appealing vision, it obscured the reality of Mexico in the post-World War II period. That Mexico was a society in which small numbers of people owned and controlled industry, commerce, communications, and finance. Similarly, a few landowners and agricultural companies dominated agriculture. Workers and peasants lost ground economically. Politics was organized for the benefit of a few powerful individuals and groups. In a sense, politics became a game in which those few privileged players earned a rich reward. The majority were not players and gained only occasional scraps, generally around election time.

In 1947 the economist Daniel Cosío Villegas published an article called "The Crisis of Mexico," in which he announced the "death" of the Mexican Revolution. There seems little doubt that it did die, or rather was murdered by the real life counterparts of Carlos Fuentes's eponymous fictional creation, Artemio Cruz, in the 1940s and 1950s. What is striking, though, is the manner in which those who murdered it embalmed the revolution and put it on display in much the same way Lenin's corpse was displayed in the mausoleum in Red Square. Mass politics continued to be a feature, largely ritualistic, of Mexican life. Educational opportunities led to the growth of a middle class. Labor unions continued to seek, within limits, a better life for their members.

A stable political system worked with only the occasional hitch until the 1980s, when a slow unraveling of the economy began. Revolutionary institutions, symbols, and rhetoric imperfectly disguised the hollowing out of the revolution.

Conclusion

In many respects the long reign of the PRI was a brilliant, if deeply flawed, achievement. It provided stability and continuity for decades. Insiders in the system lived well. Those outside the system received handouts. It is ironic that the Mexican Revolution in its institutionalized form became the basis for a highly sterile political life for several decades. In this sense, the use of power led nowhere or only back to a new version of the Porfirean era. In that regard, it must be regarded as a failure.

The Mexican Revolution was not, of course, the only revolution to be embalmed and put on display. It was, however, perhaps the one most skill-fully used for that purpose in the twentieth century. As will be seen, both the Russian and the Vietnamese, after far more bloodshed and violence, also embalmed their revolutions in systems that mocked the original ideals of the revolutions. The same could be said of revolution in China and Cuba. The Mexican Revolution managed to reach a kind of halfway house with the idealism and radicalism of the Cardenas era of the 1930s. Had Carlos Salinas de Gotari resembled Mikhail Gorbachev more closely in his reform-mindedness, perhaps the revolution might have finally achieved a stage allowing for indefinite political evolution.

It remains to be seen whether the institutions and arrangements now in place in Mexico after the election of Vicente Fox in 2000 as president will lend themselves to any kind of evolutionary refashioning of politics and economics. Perhaps Mexico in the twenty-first century can recapture a useful version of the Mexican Revolution of the twentieth century or perhaps it will find a way to leave behind the corpse of that revolution in the creation of some new basis for politics and government.

Further reading

Azuela, Mariano (1963) *The Underdogs, A Novel of the Mexican Revolution*. New York: New American Library.

Brunk, Samuel (1995) *Emiliano Zapata! Revolution and Betrayal in Mexico*. Lincoln: University of Nebraska Press.

Gonzales, Michael J. (2002) *The Mexican Revolution, 1910–1940*. Albuquerque: University of New Mexico Press.

Hall, Linda B. (1981) *Alvaro Obregon: Power and Revolution in Mexico, 1911 to 1920*. College Station: Texas A & M Press.

Hart, John Mason (1987) *Revolutionary Mexico: The Coming and Process of the Mexican Revolution*. Berkeley and Los Angeles: University of California Press.

Katz, Friedrich (1998) *The Life and Times of Pancho Villa*. Stanford, CA: Stanford University Press.

Knight, Alan (1986) *The Mexican Revolution, 1910–1920*, 2 volumes. Cambridge: Cambridge University Press.

Meyer, Michael C. (1995) *Mexican Rebel: Pascual Orozco and the Mexican Revolution, 1910–1915*. Lincoln: University of Nebraska Press.

Ross, Stanley (1955) *Francisco I. Madero, Apostle of Mexican Democracy*. New York: Columbia University Press.

Womack, John, Jr. (1968) *Zapata and the Mexican Revolution*. New York: Vintage, 1968.

Chapter 4

The Russian Revolution

The Russian Revolution is one of the seminal events of the twentieth century. Like the French Revolution, it continued to reverberate long after it had ceased its active phase. Even now, more than a decade after the collapse of its chief product, the Soviet Union, its influence still lingers.

It was, together with the Mexican Revolution and similar events in the Ottoman Empire, Persia, and China, part of a cluster of revolutions with somewhat comparable causes and aims. The impact of the Russian Revolution, however, was far greater than the other revolutions in the cluster. In many ways, it set the standard for revolution in the twentieth century, just as the French Revolution had done for the nineteenth century. Vladimir Lenin, with his ideas about a party of professional revolutionaries and the possibilities of an alliance between proletariat and peasantry, seemingly charted the path one took in order to seize power. Josif Stalin, Lenin's disciple and successor, showed how power might be used to construct an industrialized, urbanized society capable of defending and extending the revolution.

There are at least two general issues that should be addressed before considering the Russian Revolution in detail. One is the question of inevitability, a kind of Russian version of *Sonderweg*, the idea often broached in German historiography of a special historical path taken by that nation. The short answer to the question of inevitability is that the Russian Empire had many options open to it other than revolution, certainly down to and even during World War I. Political figures made strenuous efforts to modify or reform it in the twenty-five years before the outbreak of war. Even as late as the fall of 1917, there were a number of options available.

Secondly, any definition of the Russian Revolution should go beyond merely the events of the extraordinary year 1917. Instead we should view it as involving four different periods, each of which is a part of a much larger whole. First, the Russian Revolution of 1905 brought about a series of events that might have led in other circumstances to a Russian empire modified as a true constitutional monarchy. Had the changes produced by the Revolution of 1905 taken hold, the Russian Empire might have survived the trauma of World War I and possibly achieved roughly the same degree of industrialization and urbanization by the 1930s that the Soviet Union did, and at a much lower cost in human lives. Next is the crisis year of 1914. Third is 1917 and the Civil War that followed that remarkable year. Finally, there are the efforts to use power, first in the 1920s and then, a far darker picture, in the Stalin Revolution of the 1930s.

The Russian Revolution of 1905

There are intriguing similarities between the Russian Revolution of 1905 and the Mexican Revolution. Both countries were experiencing rapid but uneven economic growth based on an influx of foreign capital, circumstances that created severe problems for the working class and for the peasantry. The central government became increasingly powerful. Additionally, elites either saw their interests threatened or wanted the state to pay more attention to their particular needs and interests.

The differences, however, are also important if we want to understand more fully what led to revolution in each country. In Mexico the unresolved constitutional questions created an opening for discussion and organization. National pride and patriotism were also major factors. Ideologies played a larger role in Russia. To many Russians, it appeared that only a violent and revolutionary approach could challenge the oppressive power of the tsar. Nationalism became a factor only when the Russian Empire became involved in conflict with Japan and suffered a series of embarrassing defeats.

At the turn of the century, the Russian Empire had gambled and lost. It had gambled that the economic policies of Count Sergei Witte, the finance minister, would prove successful before the burden of taxation created an opposition to those policies. Witte had attempted to industrialize the Russian economy by attracting foreign investment, just as Mexico had done, and also by constructing the necessary infrastructure for industry and commerce. The Trans-Siberian railroad was only the most visible instance of the latter effort. The Russian economy grew rapidly in the 1890s, but, then, at the very end of the century fell into recession.

Over the next few years strikes and unemployment among the working class combined with peasant land hunger in the countryside to create a volatile mix of social disorder. On top of this, a range of ideologies challenged the tsarist system politically. Liberal professionals wanted a political system more responsive to their particular kind of expertise, one in which they as educated men and women could participate. Marxists worked to organize the working class and to spread the ideas of Marx and Engels within the Russian Empire. They looked to the fall of the empire, expecting to help bring about a bourgeois democracy within which they could continue to work toward the ultimate goal of a proletarian revolution and then a classless society. The Socialist Revolutionaries worked among the peasantry and looked to an alternate path that would eliminate any need to imitate the West. They were largely responsible for the campaigns of assassination that contributed to an atmosphere of lawlessness and disorder in the Russian Empire by 1904.

It is likely the Russian Empire would have weathered this particularly rough period except for the Russo-Japanese War that began in 1904. Defeats suffered during the war called into question the effectiveness of the tsarist government. Commitment of troops and matériel to the war effort also made it difficult for the regime to respond effectively to the outbreak of revolution in 1905.

The catalyst for the revolution was an event in January 1905 later known as "Bloody Sunday." Father Georgi Gapon led a group of workers, their wives, and children to the Winter Palace in St. Petersburg to present a petition to the tsar, and the authorities responded by firing on the crowd. The massacre of peaceful demonstrators set off a spontaneous revolutionary movement that the government could not deal with effectively. In the major cities, radical students, liberal professionals, and workers met together to discuss events. In St. Petersburg, a *Soviet* or council – a broadly representative body – was formed. Its main goal was the creation of a *Duma*, a national parliamentary body.

In August the government called for a Duma with which it would consult on policy issues. The Duma would, however, have no legislative powers. In September railroad workers began what quickly turned into a paralyzing general strike. Count Witte presented the tsar with two options: use force to repress the revolution or issue a manifesto promising a Duma. When Tsar Nicholas II realized that no one was willing to repress the movement through the use of force, he agreed to the October Manifesto, a document that granted a Duma and basic civil rights, together with the promise to issue other laws later.

The October Manifesto split the revolutionary opposition into those who believed they had gained what they wanted – a constitution, representative government, and elections – and those who wanted to continue the revolution to the point of overthrowing the tsarist regime. The brief period in which the liberal upper and middle classes allied with the lower classes ended. In its place were possibilities for the tsarist government to work with liberals in the establishment of a constitutional monarchy that would not only fulfill political desires but also pay attention to the many social and economic issues that existed in the empire.

The crisis year of 1914

If Witte had been the key figure in the period before 1905, Piotr Stolypin was his equivalent after 1905. Debate continues to this day as to whether Stolypin's policies had any chance of changing Russia sufficiently so that it could have moved toward political freedom and an industrialized economy. It seems unlikely that his policies alone would have accomplished those ends, but it is also true that his policies did not receive anything like an adequate test. For various reasons, among them lack of consistent support from Nicholas and failure on Stolypin's part to find ways to work with the Duma, the efforts to change and reform Russia after 1905 were cut short.

Stolypin worked in three complementary directions. First, he worked in 1906 and 1907 to stamp out the last remaining fires of the revolution. By the use of field courts martial and the "Stolypin necktie" (the hangman's noose), he was able to restore order. The second policy involved taming the Duma. While Stolypin was largely successful in this aim, revising the suffrage arrangements drastically in 1907 to favor the aristocracy, he did not succeed in establishing a working relationship with the more docile Duma.

Stolypin's third policy involved another wager, this time that a peasant freed from the tyranny of the *mir* or village commune, farming his own land as a consolidated holding, and, ideally, living on that land, would become a conservative force, and a source of support for the government. If enough peasants could be turned into conservative small farmers, then a major element of revolutionary discontent in the countryside would be effectively eliminated. Legislation made it possible for peasants to petition to dissolve the mir and to consolidate their holdings. Even when this was done, however, it was not usually the case that peasants lived independently on their holdings. Since most peasants continued to live in the village, they usually remained under the influence of village traditions and customs. The self-reliant, independent farmer that Stolypin hoped to create was the exception rather than the rule.

Even before Stolypin was assassinated in 1911, he had lost the backing of the tsar. Neither Nicholas nor his advisors understood the necessity of modifying the tsarist system and the importance of strong, competent leaders. Nicholas was determined to pass on to his son what his father had passed on to him: the tsarist autocracy. With this kind of blind stubbornness leading the way, it is difficult to imagine how the Russian Empire might have found an alternate path.

Still, in 1914, while a serious crisis existed on three different levels, it would have been premature to see that the empire was doomed to revolution. The first level was cultural. Among many writers, artists, and other cultural figures there existed a sense of impending catastrophe. A vague, intuitive feeling that the Russian Empire would simply explode in the near future pervaded. Art and culture would be lost in the destruction and chaos that this would bring.

The second level was more tangible. Its focus was the intense strike movement that had begun in 1913 and assumed gigantic proportions in the first part of 1914. The government worried the movement might paralyze the economy. The Bolsheviks (the Leninist faction of the Russian Social Democratic Labor Party [RSDLP]) hoped to use the strike movement to launch a revolution. Compared with 1905, however, one key element was missing. The countryside was relatively quiet. Without a restive peasantry, it was unlikely the strike movement by itself could have led to revolution.

Finally, the third level featured a split between the *obshchestvo*, that portion of society involved in politics, and the tsarist regime. The government had long ago used up any political good will created by the October Manifesto and the hopes for a constitutional order after 1905. At the same time, the *obshchestvo* feared the masses: the workers on strike certainly, and also the peasantry.

We cannot know what might have occurred had the triple crisis of 1914 not been interrupted by the coming of war. It is doubtful, however, that the beginning of war cut short a developing revolution. Russia probably would have found some way to live through the crisis. What the war did accomplish, however, was to divert attention away from the possibility of a constructive response to the crisis. In the absence of war, perhaps Russians would have found positive steps to take. Failure to respond adequately to a crisis made the next crisis that much more difficult to deal with.

The 1917 Revolution

The February Revolution[1] ended the Romanov dynasty. It was actually more a collapse of the empire under the pressures of war than a revolution. Battered by defeats, the regime was also close to economic disintegration early in 1917. Nicholas and his ministers had not taken advantage of the desire of members of the Duma, industrialists, and professionals to aid in the war effort. Nothing like the British- and German-controlled economies existed in Russia. Instead factories lacked raw materials, city dwellers went hungry and cold, and the army lacked necessary supplies, weapons, and ammunition.

Beginning on the 23rd of February (8 March), crowds of people, a large percentage of them women, thronged the streets of Petrograd (the wartime name of St. Petersburg). Over the next several days, the crowds grew larger and more radical. The soldiers sent to control the crowds made common cause with them. Unable to maintain order in the capital, the regime disintegrated.

A Provisional Government derived from the Duma stepped into the political space that opened up. The Provisional Government issued a number of popular decrees such as one calling for the eight-hour workday. The government looked to an eventual constituent assembly to work out the details of the new system of government. Initially, however, the main task was to continue the war effort. Other pressing questions, such as land for the peasantry, were to be postponed indefinitely. Perhaps the most important mistake made by the Provisional Government was to overestimate the patience and goodwill of the masses.

Another institution, the Petrograd Soviet, appeared at the same time the Provisional Government formed. It represented the workers, soldiers, and sailors of the Petrograd area. With a constantly shifting membership, it reflected public opinion in the most direct way. While it did not try to exercise governmental power, it had considerable leverage over the Provisional Government. Observers

1 In the twentieth century the calendar in use in Russia was thirteen days behind the calendar used in the West. Thus the February Revolution took place in March and the October Revolution happened in November by the Western calendar.

spoke of "dual power": the idea that the Provisional Government had to consider opinion in the Petrograd Soviet in everything it did.

Initially, the leading figures in the Provisional Government were Pavel Miliukov, the foreign minister and a Constitutional Democrat (Kadet), and Aleksandr Guchkov, minister of war and an Octobrist. When Miliukov indicated that the government would adhere to its agreements with its allies in the war, including provisions for territorial change after the war, the ensuing uproar led to a reorganization of the government. In the new Provisional Government there were two important developments. First, Aleksandr Kerensky, the new minister of war, emerged as the leading figure. Kerensky, a moderate socialist, seemed more at home in the revolutionary chaos of 1917 than the other members of the government. The second development involved the entry of representatives from the socialist parties into the government. Both the Mensheviks, Lenin's rivals in the RSDLP, and the Socialist Revolutionaries took part in the new Provisional Government. They now shared responsibility for governmental policy and actions.

Lenin, leader of the Bolsheviks, returned to Russia in April 1917. In his "April Theses" he established a position that set his party apart from all others in Russia. He called boldly for peace without annexations or indemnities, land to the peasants, and all power to the Soviets. This was a crucial contribution to the eventual seizure of power carried out by the Bolsheviks. At the time, however, many Bolsheviks had difficulty accepting this new direction. Not for the last time, Lenin had to convince many in his party of the correctness of his views.

By the end of the summer of 1917, it appeared that Kerensky, who had become prime minister during the summer, was firmly in control of the government. Despite the failure of the offensive he had organized, the Provisional Government had come through the chaotic July Days in good shape. During that time armed demonstrators had called for the socialist parties to take charge of the government and the Bolsheviks had considered the idea of leading an attempt to seize power. The socialist parties declined to take responsibility for the government and the Bolsheviks decided to head off an armed insurrection rather than take the chance of it failing. In August an attempted coup from the Right by General Kornilov failed. The Bolshevik Party was weakened by rumors that Lenin was a German agent. Lenin fled to Finland in disguise to avoid arrest and several Bolsheviks were taken into custody.

In the fall neither Kerensky nor Lenin saw the Russian situation very clearly. Circumstances worked out in favor of Lenin, however. Kerensky continued to delay the election of the Constituent Assembly by convening groups that were meant to represent public opinion and prepare for the elections. Lenin, for his part, had convinced himself that Russia was ripe for revolution. He set about the business of convincing others this was the case. The Central Committee (CC) of the Bolshevik Party was reluctant to take action, but agreed finally to put the idea of revolution on the agenda.

Two factors helped the Bolsheviks gain power in the October Revolution. The first was the chaotic conditions in the country. Russia was in a state of near anarchy with peasants seizing land, workers occupying factories, soldiers deserting their units, and national minorities working toward autonomy or even independence. Towns and regions responded to local situations without much reference to Petrograd. At the same time, they looked to Petrograd for what national leadership was available. The second factor was the work of Leon Trotsky, now a major figure in the Bolshevik Party and an influential member of the Petrograd Soviet. Trotsky used his position in the Soviet to make preparations to protect the revolution. He established connections with Red Guard units, workers' militias, and the soldiers and sailors in the area, undermining the authority of the Provisional Government over the military units as he did so.

The Bolsheviks presented the Provisional Government's actions against *Pravda*, the Bolshevik newspaper, as the beginning of a counter-revolution. Very quickly, they established control in Petrograd and overthrew the Provisional Government. The Bolshevik Party was still a minority party, even in Petrograd, but they could claim their goals were broadly representative of the goals of the masses in the country. Most workers and peasants were not Bolsheviks, but they agreed with the Bolshevik program, particularly with the idea of defending the revolution. The Bolshevik takeover was presented to the Second All-Russian Congress of Soviets, then just beginning to meet in Petrograd, as an effort to preserve the revolution. Not all the delegates were willing to sanction what the Bolsheviks had done and many walked out of the Congress. The rump, however, approved a Bolshevik–Left Socialist Revolutionary government.

The seizure of power had been accomplished with relatively little bloodshed. The Civil War that followed was bloody and cruel. It has been argued that the Civil War period was that point at which the revolution began to go in the wrong direction. Steps taken and methods adopted then made it difficult in later years to avoid the harsh regime that Stalin installed in the 1930s.

Initially, several difficult choices had to be made. The first concerned the Constituent Assembly, which met for the first and last time in January 1918. About a quarter of the delegates was Bolshevik. Others came from the Left SRs, but most of the delegates were moderate SRs and Mensheviks. The Bolsheviks unceremoniously dissolved the Constituent Assembly once they had a sense of how difficult it would be to work with it.

Another difficult choice concerned the question of whether to sign a peace treaty with Germany. Although Trotsky tried some clever maneuvers ("no peace, no war"), the Germans imposed harsh terms in the Treaty of Brest-Litovsk and Lenin insisted on the necessity of accepting the treaty.

"War Communism," the set of economic policies that prevailed from 1918 to 1921, was in large part a response to the conditions of the Civil War, the necessity of controlling food supplies, industrial production, and the distribution of goods. It is also true, however, that War Communism was an effort to construct a single economic plan and to create the institutional basis for Communism. Although it failed as a method of organizing and managing the economy, Bolshevik experience with decision-making and use of force helped to convince them of the necessity of coercion in shaping the new society.

The activities of the White Armies and the several instances of foreign intervention also helped shape a siege mentality that continued to characterize the party even after the end of the Civil War. The creation of the Red Army under Trotsky and the *Cheka*, the secret police, under Feliks Dzerzhinskii, also contributed to an atmosphere in which brutal methods seemed necessary. Lenin had always prided himself on being "hard" rather than "soft." The times seemed to require that the Bolsheviks exhibit toughness and show a willingness to use whatever means were available and likely to gain results.

Some European socialists criticized the Bolsheviks for holding on to power at all costs. Rosa Luxemburg, for example, a founder of the German Communist Party, wondered if it would not be better to relinquish power rather than use such drastic methods to preserve it. The Civil War was in any case a formative experience for millions of Russians, whether party members or not. In addition to toughening many who gained positions of power in the 1920s, it also created a revolutionary myth that found a response in the idealism and willingness to sacrifice for the goals of the revolution that characterized many young Russians at the end of the 1920s. Stalin tapped into that energy and enthusiasm during the Five-Year Plans.

NEP and the 1920s

Soviet Russia in 1921 was a different country from the empire that had entered World War I in 1914. It had lost territory in the course of the war. Millions had died during the war and Civil War and more would die in the famine that was beginning. Many of the aristocracy and parts of the middle classes had emigrated. Sailors were revolting on the island of Kronstadt, formerly a hotbed of Bolshevik support. Peasant rebellion flared up in many provinces. Even the working class, in whose name the Bolsheviks had seized power, was far from united in its support. The economy was in a shambles, industrial production at a fraction of 1913 levels, and land under cultivation at a level perhaps half of what it had been before the war.

At the Tenth Party Congress that year Lenin convinced the party to accept a strategic retreat. The New Economic Policy (NEP) ended War Communism and allowed for a partial return of capitalism to Russia. Under the policy, the government collected a percentage of peasant produce. The more the peasants produced, the larger the surplus they would have to market themselves. Small shops and retail establishments were allowed to do business again. The government controlled the "commanding heights" of the economy:

such sectors as wholesale and foreign trade, banking, insurance, and large-scale manufacturing. The idea was to provide some incentive to encourage people, especially the peasantry, to increase production. This would lead to the recovery of the overall economy.

The intriguing question is what Lenin would have done had he not died in 1924. Some of his articles, "Better Fewer, But Better," for example, suggest a gradualism, an evolutionary approach. While that article touched on several themes, it clearly suggested that more careful work might lead to genuine accomplishments. It was better not to try to do everything at once.

Lenin also spoke of a "cultural revolution," in this case emphasizing literacy as a prerequisite for acquainting Russians with Bolshevik methods and goals. At times he seemed to believe that a generation might pass before the basis for Communism would be at hand. Of course, he had moments of enthusiasm: when American work methods, or the spread of electrical power, or the introduction of the tractor into the countryside would quickly prepare the way for the fulfillment of revolutionary goals.

It is impossible to know what Lenin would have done had he remained in good health. It is, however, difficult to imagine him waiting patiently year after year for a cultural revolution of some sort to take hold. As it happened, Lenin's death in 1924 led to a struggle for power.

The images of the French Revolution continued to exert a strong influence in the Soviet Russia of the 1920s. The many Bolsheviks who were familiar with that revolution constantly looked over their shoulders to see where their revolution was in relation to the French Revolution. At first, the concern was mainly whether Trotsky was a man on horseback, a Napoleon, who might bring about a Russian 18th of Brumaire (when Napoleon seized power according to the revolutionary calendar in use at the time). Trotsky, for all his brilliance and organizing ability, proved to be not particularly astute politically. He allowed the troika of Grigori Zinoviev, Lev Kamenev, and Stalin to reduce his power and either dismiss many of his allies or send them on assignments where they could not actively aid him.

Stalin used a measure against factionalism passed at the Tenth Party Congress in 1921 to attack Trotsky on several occasions. He also used his powers of patronage to create allies and weaken potential opponents. The Lenin Enrollment of 1924 swelled the ranks of the party with new recruits. More and more, new members of the party gained their understanding of Marxism–Leninism from Stalin's speeches and writings. Stalin became the high priest of the Lenin cult. Perhaps most important, Stalin set the agendas for meetings of the Politburo, the chief executive body of the party and source of real power in the country, and controlled much of the information it used in making decisions. As General Secretary, he influenced the work of many other party and government agencies. His letters to Vyacheslav Molotov, his right-hand man in the 1920s and 1930s, are filled with Stalin's assessments of political situations and assignments for Molotov to carry out. They show how much energy and intelligence Stalin put into consolidating his power and setting the agenda for the Soviet Union.

The troika fell apart and Stalin took center stage after he announced in 1925 his slogan of "Socialism in One Country," one that was widely popular. It went against the assumption, associated with Trotsky, that the Russian Revolution would spark revolutions in more advanced countries, which would then aid the Soviet Union in completing the work of the revolution. Stalin allied next with Nikolai Bukharin, a former supporter of War Communism who had more recently become a spokesman for Lenin's ideas of gradualism. Stalin and Bukharin used the power of the party and government to quash the attempts by Trotsky, Zinoviev, and Kamenev to stage independent celebrations of the tenth anniversary of the Russian Revolution in 1927.

While the political struggle raged over which leader in the Communist Party would control and use power, the Soviet Union enjoyed a remarkable decade of cultural and intellectual ferment. The tragedy of the 1920s in the Soviet Union is that there existed tremendous potential for revolution but not nearly enough resources to accomplish it. And eventually, much of the potential would be destroyed or at least silenced.

A case in point is *Vkhutemas* (the Higher State Art–Technical Studio), established in Moscow to train students in architecture, sculpture, graphics, woodwork, textiles, metalwork, and painting. It was very much like its German counterpart, the Bauhaus movement, in terms of curriculum and interest in art and technology. In the 1920s it was for some years arguably the most advanced art school in the world, but it lacked the resources available to the Bauhaus. The impoverished society and economy within which it existed could not sustain it.

Another example was *Proletkult*, a workers' educational organization with prewar roots. It set out in the 1920s to create a new working-class culture that would replace the old bourgeois culture. This led mostly to the destruction of existing works of art. The attempt to create worker poets and novelists, as opposed to attempts to educate members of the working class, was not very successful. Nonetheless, a theme for the 1920s was the need for a proletarian culture to match the new political arrangements.

Vladimir Mayakovsky is an interesting individual example. A Futurist poet and a playwright, Mayakovsky had impeccable credentials as an avant-garde artist. He also attempted to lend his poetry and other talents to the revolution in more direct ways. One was writing jingles for *Rosta*, the Russian telegraphic agency. These were used with posters to acquaint people with the virtues of brushing their teeth or changing their underwear. One of Mayakovsky's plays, *The Bedbug*, imagined a distant and sterile future in which a Soviet citizen from the 1920s, somewhat crude and unrefined, reappeared along with a bed-bug. A satire on some of the tendencies of the 1920s toward increased regulation and control, Mayakovsky's point was that the official revolution might squeeze the life out of society. He committed suicide in 1930, in part from frustration with the communist bureaucracy, and in part because of romance that had not worked out.

Evgeny Zamyatin is another example. His dystopian novel, *We*, projects a future of complete conformism. In his essays, Zamyatin wrote about the usefulness of heretics, such as Copernicus or Galileo. It was crucial in his view to keep asking questions. According to him there should never be a final answer. The revolution should never be finished.

The Stalin Revolution of the 1930s

The wealth of talent, inspired thinking, and social concern that characterized the 1920s was mostly squandered in the 1930s in the heavy-handed approach to industrialization and urbanization in the Soviet Union. Behind these efforts, not yet the supremely powerful figure he would soon become, was Stalin. In 1929 Stalin was 50 years old. The celebration of this milestone in his life was unprecedented. Soviet newspapers contained greetings and congratulations from all parts of the Soviet Union. Associates organized a number of special events to recognize the occasion. While it was still a few years before the beginnings of the cult of personality used to glorify him in the 1930s, Stalin was starting to view himself as a rival to Lenin, not merely as his disciple.

In 1929 Stalin could take advantage of the genuine enthusiasm of many Soviet citizens for the First Five-Year Plan. The ideas of a "Second October" and of completing the work of the Civil War were popular, especially among the urban working class. Many younger Communists, those who had not participated in 1917 or in the Civil War, liked the idea of having a chance to show their revolutionary enthusiasm, dedication, and willingness to sacrifice. The main idea of the plan was to provide the economic basis for socialism. Comprehensive economic planning, a concept Soviet officials had studied extensively in the 1920s, was supposed to make it possible to marshal the resources of the country and use them to industrialize the economy.

Many liked the idea of making the Soviet Union into a great power once again. Stalin emphasized the need to prepare militarily in particular and in 1931 he gave a famous and prescient speech. In it he noted that the Soviet Union had ten years to prepare if it did not want to experience the same kinds of beatings Russians had experienced in the past at the hands of the Mongols, the Poles, the Swedes, and the Germans. Additionally, many Communists saw a chance to bring jobs and revenue to their district by locating a new hydroelectric plant or tractor factory there. Others hoped to advance their career by actively participating in the Five-Year Plan. It was also of no small importance that a project such as the Five-Year Plan required a strong Communist Party and strong leaders at the head of that party.

Stalin saw the world in terms of "Kto–kogo" or who–whom: Who got the best of whom, who was on top, who on bottom. His intention was to remain on top (and increasingly to rival Lenin as a great leader). He wanted also the

Communist Party to remain in charge and the Soviet Union to become a great power, capable of defending the revolution. Those who believed in the Five-Year Plan also saw Stalin as a capable administrator, the kind of person who could make such a plan work. Many of the other communist leaders seemed, by comparison, dreamers, unwilling to do the difficult work necessary to yank the nation into the twentieth century.

The First Five-Year Plan officially dated from the latter part of 1928. It called originally for difficult but not impossible goals, but Stalin insisted on raising goals to ridiculous levels. In several cases, goals were repeatedly revised. Another problem concerned what some called the "Bolshevik tempo." This was a problem Lenin had noted a decade earlier. If something could be accomplished in a year, better to do it in six months. Also, the party seemed to believe the larger the project the better. Magnitogorsk, the new metallurgical complex near the southern end of the Ural Mountains, was a good example of both "Bolshevik tempo" and the tendency to favor the gigantic. It was also an excellent example of the inefficiency and waste connected with many projects in the Five-Year Plan. For example, a piece of expensive machinery might arrive and the building it was supposed to occupy was yet to be constructed. While construction proceeded, the machine would be set in a field and left to rust.

Nevertheless, the Soviet Union became a major industrial power in the 1930s, capable of manufacturing a broad range of modern products. The labor force more than doubled, growing from approximately eleven and a half million to nearly twenty-three million. A large number of peasants left the new collective farms to enter the labor force. Women also entered the labor force in large numbers. These were elements of a demographic transition that made the Soviet Union a more urban society than it had been a decade earlier, with a large working class and also a larger middle class. Rapid social mobility and extreme social dislocation were two prominent features of the period. Consumer goods, however, were scarce. Housing was crowded and often substandard. Soviet citizens looked to a future when various luxuries and novelties would be taken for granted. They also read avidly about heroes, Stakhanovite workers (workers who fulfilled their work quotas many times over), aviators, polar explorers, and, of course, Comrade Stalin.

The growth of industry, especially heavy industry, and the use of centralized economic planning were the two most important elements of the Five-Year Plan. Collectivization, the third component, changed the countryside drastically. The goal of collectivization was increased productivity in agriculture. In theory at least, collective farms, furnished with agricultural machinery, tractors, and combines, would benefit from economies of scale. Increased productivity would free some peasants to join the labor force and also create a grain surplus that could be marketed abroad to help pay for industrialization.

The reality was a disaster. Collectivization began in 1928, supposedly as a voluntary process with modest goals. By early 1930 about 50 percent of peasant families had joined collective farms, often forced to do so by armed groups recruited from the cities. The level of resistance grew so high that Stalin published an article in March 1930, "Dizzy with Success," in which he blamed problems on overzealous subordinates and reassured peasants they would not be forced to join. Although many left then, continual pressure resulted in over 90 percent of peasant families joining collective or state farms by 1933.

One major feature of collectivization was the hunt for the *kulak* (a word meaning fist but also used to refer to the so-called rich peasant). Often this person was simply one of the best farmers in the village, someone with some independence and initiative. Occasionally those identified as kulaks were shot on the spot. More often they were given a short time to pack a few belongings and then shipped off to some desolate spot to start all over again. The net result of this very arbitrary process was that many of the best farmers left the collective, whether to join the forces of industry or to go into a kind of exile.

Collectivization was the major economic failure of the Five-Year Plan. It led directly to a massive famine in 1932 in the Ukraine and the northern Caucasus region. As a result, perhaps seven million peasants died, in large part because Stalin would not admit that famine conditions existed or allow relief efforts. Collectivization also resulted in peasants killing several million animals rather than surrendering them to the collective. The promised tractors and other kinds of agricultural machinery remained in short supply.

The Stalin Revolution did not originally include the idea of purges or what came to be called the Terror. In fact, there was some resistance to the idea of using it against members of the party even as late as the beginning of the worst part of the Terror, the *Yezhovshchina* (named after Yezhov, the head of the NKVD or secret police during the Terror) in early 1937. The trials of foreigners and so-called bourgeois specialists in the early part of the Five-Year Plan had been a way of finding scapegoats for the failures of the plan. The Terror was a massive campaign directed in large part against many of the party and government officials most closely associated with the Five-Year Plans. It also seemed designed to eliminate any source of opposition to Stalin.

The beginnings of the Terror are conventionally dated from the 1934 assassination of Sergei Kirov, the popular leader of the Communist Party in Leningrad (formerly St. Petersburg) and a member of the ruling Politburo of the Communist Party. Stalin may have had Kirov assassinated. At the seventeenth Party Congress in 1934 Stalin had been embarrassed by the number of negative votes he had received in the election for the Central Committee of the party as compared to Kirov. Whoever was responsible for Kirov's death, the attempt to assign blame led eventually to the first show trial in 1936, a trial featuring Zinoviev and Kamenev. Both had once been allies of Stalin. What seems likely is a kind of snowball effect, in which subordinates tried to prove their loyalty by rounding up supporters of Zinoviev, Kamenev, and the person viewed as the major threat to Soviet Communism, Trotsky. Stalin and his close supporters perhaps began to believe their own propaganda about the abundance of enemies and foreign agents and determined to remove any possible threat to their power. This would help to explain the massive purge of the army in 1937.

The number of people affected by the Terror remains controversial: did millions die in the purges or in the concentration camps of the *Gulag* (the acronym for the prison system of the secret police)? While attempts to determine the number continue today, it appears the NKVD executed almost a million prisoners during the purges, while many others died in the Gulag over the remainder of the Stalin era. It would appear, however, that estimates of ten million or more are simply too high.

In an interesting paradox, the Stalin Revolution also operated as a counter-revolution. Trotsky saw the 1930s as the "Soviet Thermidor," a reference to the simultaneous end of Robespierre's power and the Terror in the French Revolution. While the Stalin Revolution resulted in important demographic, social, and economic changes that might be considered revolutionary, it also brought about cultural and behavioral changes that harked back to the past and cannot be considered revolutionary at all. It first created a privileged group of bureaucrats in the party, government, industry, science, military, and other important areas. They moved far away from anything resembling equality or a proletarian lifestyle. The elite had access to special supplies of food, separate medical care, their own apartment buildings, palatial resorts, *dachas* (vacation cottages) in the countryside, and chauffeur-driven automobiles. While not an aristocracy in the same way as the nobility had been in imperial Russia, they lived very different kinds of lives from those of average Soviet citizens. The education system offers another example, one that affected elites and non-elites alike. The experimental approaches of the 1920s were dropped in the 1930s in favor of disciplined classrooms, rote learning, school uniforms, and other trappings of the tsarist educational system.

The emphasis in the Soviet Union in the 1930s was on a middle-class approach to living. This meant that women hung curtains on the windows, put out proper place settings for dinner, men wore suits and ties, and all had at least a superficial acquaintance with high culture. Workers had access to free education and health care. They also enjoyed low-cost housing and subsidized food prices. Those who remained in the countryside, often the very young and the very old, were the major losers in the new Soviet Union.

Conclusion

Like the Mexican and the British Revolution before it, the Russian Revolution was episodic. The 1917 Revolution was a key element in the longer revolutionary process, but not the only element. The 1905 Revolution and the failure to take advantage of the possibilities that it had produced prepared the way for 1917 and the Civil War period. Those who controlled Russia after 1917 used the 1920s to consolidate power and recover from earlier events, as was the case with the Mexican Revolution. They then moved in a far more radical fashion to remake Soviet Russia in the 1930s.

The results in both Mexico and the Soviet Union contrast strongly with the results of the British Revolution. The British Revolution created conditions that allowed for the evolution to a more flexible if hardly perfect system of government, economy, and society. There were moments in both the eighteenth and nineteenth centuries when the evolving constitutional monarchy in Britain seemed jeopardized. Nonetheless, the British system avoided the repetition of revolution even when it experienced disorder and protest. The Mexican and Soviet Revolutions, however, created relatively inflexible systems that worked reasonably well for the 1940s and 1950s, less well in the 1960s and 1970s, then badly in the 1980s (and 1990s for Mexico). The different parts of the old Soviet Union continue to struggle with the transition that began with the collapse of the Soviet Union in 1991.

By the end of the 1930s life in the Soviet Union, while sometimes reminiscent of the tsarist empire, was radically different from what had existed before World War I. (The impact of World War II on the Soviet Union was profound. Some scholars see it as equivalent to the impact of Stalin's policies in the 1930s. Whatever the merits of that perspective, it lies outside the scope of this discussion.) While the party leaders who followed Stalin lacked his immense and arbitrary power, the system still depended heavily on a single, powerful leader. Even when that leader could barely function, as was the case with Leonid Brezhnev in his last years, the system was so constructed that his symbolic presence was necessary.

Less visible was the Communist Party bureaucracy and the several other associated bureaucracies. Composed of elites with power and privilege, they, more than any other aspect of the system, stifled initiative and innovation. While it may be true that the gap between the elites and the masses was less in the Soviet Union than it is in capitalist societies, there was still a considerable gap that flew in the face of the teachings of Marx and Engels. And the system produced an economy that had little motivation to innovate or even to improve what was already being done. Only in a few areas, usually associated with military matters or cultural prestige, did the Soviet Union excel. In many rather basic areas, particularly consumer goods and housing, and, later, health care, it did poorly.

For the average Soviet citizen, the revolution that had played itself out by the end of the 1930s had two attractive features: it had produced a powerful state, the proof of which was the Soviet victory over Nazi Germany in World War II, and it had created a badly managed welfare state that provided most of the necessities of life, either at no cost or at low, subsidized prices. In return, the citizen was required to conform to the patterns set by the system. He or she might find a small area in which it was possible to be an individual and have some limited control over a portion of one's life. Relatively few protested or rebelled, although there was more of that sort of thing than the regime admitted. Also, by the late 1960s the phenomenon of the dissident working his or her contacts with Western journalists had emerged.

Compared with the Mexican Revolution, the Russian Revolution was bloodier, more brutal, and more repressive. It was also far more influential. Lenin's ideas about revolutionaries and the revolutionary party influenced Marxists and other radical thinkers and activists throughout the twentieth century. Stalin's concept of the Five-Year Plan found echoes in the newly emerging nations of the Third World and even in Western Europe. The Soviet Union's role in World War II appeared to vindicate the system. Then, during the Cold War, the Soviet Union offered what struck many as an appealing alternative to rapacious and neo-colonial capitalism. Even as the Soviet Union was visibly failing in the 1980s, it continued to play a major role in world affairs.

In the end, the Russian Revolution may be compared most fruitfully with the French Revolution. Like the French Revolution, it introduced new institutions and procedures into politics, transforming the practice of politics and international relations, even in those countries that resisted its influence. While not the leading power of the twentieth century, as France had been the leading power of the eighteenth century, it was sufficiently powerful so that it formed a disturbing presence on the international scene, especially after World War II when the world became for a time largely a bipolar world. It helped to create a world in which revolutions, as different ways of doing politics, no longer had any chance of playing themselves out with relatively little outside interference. After the Russian Revolution, great powers and especially the United States paid the closest attention to the phenomenon of revolution wherever it might appear.

Finally, the twentieth century was a century marked by the rise of social engineering as a major approach to governmental and economic affairs. The Russian Revolution, in all its permutations, offered an example of the most radical approaches to social engineering in the century, matched or exceeded only perhaps by the Chinese Revolution after the Communists took power there in 1949 or by the madness of the Khmer Rouge in Cambodia in the 1970s. Unfortunately, for millions of Russians, the Russian Communist Party had sufficient power and resources to attempt to create new revolutionary men and women. What had been in France largely plans and schemes became a nightmarish reality in the Soviet Union. In the end, the Russian Revolution may be seen as a costly, flawed and utopian project based on a fundamental misreading of human nature.

Further reading

1917

Acton, Edward, Cherniaev, Vladimir Iu., and Rosenberg, William G. (editors) (1997) *Critical Companion to the Russian Revolution, 1914–1921*. Bloomington and Indianapolis: Indiana University Press.

Carr, E. H. (1950, 1952, 1953) *The Bolshevik Revolution, 1917–1923*, 3 volumes. London: Macmillan.

Daniels, Robert V. (1967) *Red October: The Bolshevik Revolution of 1917*. New York: Scribner.

Fitzpatrick, Sheila (1994) *The Russian Revolution*, second edition. Oxford and New York: Oxford University Press.

Hasegawa, Tsuyoshi (1981) *The February Revolution, Petrograd, 1917*. Seattle: University of Washington Press.

Keep, John H. L. (1976) *The Russian Revolution: A Study in Mass Mobilization*. New York: W. W. Norton.

Koenker, Diane (1981) *Moscow Workers and the 1917 Revolution*. Princeton, NJ: Princeton University Press.

Rabinowitch, Alexander (1968) *Prelude to Revolution: The Petrograd Bolsheviks and the July 1917 Uprising*. Bloomington: Indiana University Press.

—— (1976) *The Bolsheviks Come to Power: The Revolution of 1917 in Petrograd*. New York: W. W. Norton.

The Stalinist Revolution

Brooks, Jeffrey (2000) *Thank You, Comrade Stalin! Soviet Public Culture from Revolution to Cold War*. Princeton, NJ: Princeton University Press.

Conquest, Robert (1986) *The Harvest of Sorrow: Soviet Collectivization and the Terror-Famine*. New York and Oxford: Oxford University Press.

Davies, R. W. (1980, 1989, 1996) *The Industrialization of Soviet Russia*, 4 volumes. Cambridge, MA: Harvard University Press.

Fitzpatrick, Sheila (1999) *Everyday Stalinism. Ordinary Life in Extraordinary Times: Soviet Russia in the 1930s*. Oxford: Oxford University Press.

Kotkin, Stephen (1995) *Magnetic Mountain*. Berkeley: University of California Press.

Rosenberg, W. G. and Siegelbaum, L. H. (editors) (1993) *Social Dimensions of Soviet Industrialization*. Bloomington: Indiana University Press.

Siegelbaum, L. H. (1986) *Stakhanovism and the Politics of Productivity in the USSR, 1935–1941*. Cambridge, MA: Harvard University Press.

—— and Sokolov, Andrei (editors) (2000) *Stalinism as a Way of Life: A Narrative in Documents*. New Haven, CT, and London: Yale University Pres.

Tucker, Robert C. (1990) *Stalin in Power: The Revolution from Above, 1928–1941*. New York: W.W. Norton.

Chapter 5

The Vietnamese Revolution

The Vietnamese Revolution is a study in endurance and perseverance. The Vietnamese fought the French between 1946 and 1954, and then a South Vietnamese regime backed by the United States between 1960 and 1975. Victory came only at the end of a long and brutal struggle.

Although the Vietnamese Communists led the revolution in its different phases, and dominated the fronts that sought to rally broad support, the major focus was always national liberation and unification. The fronts sponsored by the Communists often emphasized a program of social and economic change in the countryside, but this depended on the occasion and the audience. Vietnamese Communists gave other elements of the Marxist agenda relatively little attention so long as liberation and unification were the major goals of the revolution.

The Vietnamese Revolution is a prime example of post-World War II national liberation movements. It is also one of the few successful, communist-led movements. Commentators have explained its success in many ways: Vietnamese reactions to the brutality of the French colonial administration; the long tradition of Vietnamese resistance to imperialism; the charismatic leadership of Ho Chi Minh; the organizational advantage afforded by the Leninist party organization; aid from Communist China; and the short-sightedness of Vietnamese elites in the south, among others. An investigation of the Vietnamese Revolution will help explain its success. The investigation may also clarify the reasons for different outcomes in other national liberation movements in the postwar period.

The Vietnamese Revolution had a major international impact. In this regard, it ranks with the Russian, Chinese, and Iranian Revolutions as the most influential of the twentieth century. In the 1960s it seemed the best example of a people struggling for freedom and national sovereignty. Che Guevara's idea of "Two, Three, Many Vietnams," that is, a multiplication of national liberation struggles and other efforts to expand freedom, appealed to many in the First World, the urban, industrialized world that included the United States and Western Europe. Many wanted to find outlets for their idealism, for what in some cases might be called a revolutionary romanticism. The Vietnam War, which the Vietnamese call the American War, played a major role in causing Americans to question not simply government policy but also values and basic principles of American life.

Just as the Spanish Civil War seemed to be a touchstone for differing political ideologies in the 1930s, so the struggle of the Vietnamese caused people in many parts of the world to line up behind Democracy or Communism. It caused people to divide the world into the forces of good and those of evil. And like Spain in the 1930s, Vietnam was engulfed in a national tragedy of immense dimensions.

Vietnam and Indochina

Indochina was an artificial creation of French imperialism developed between approximately 1860 and 1890. It consisted of Vietnam, divided into the two protectorates of Tonkin in the north and Annam in the center, and the colony of Cochin China in the south, plus Cambodia and Laos. Vietnam, which had been both an empire and an anti-imperialist nation (with reference to the Chinese Empire) in the preceding thousand years, ceased to exist. Throughout the 1890s and the first decade of the twentieth century, the Vietnamese elite attempted to use force to resist the French colonial regime. In a time when the old rules no longer prevailed (the Vietnamese presented it as a time when "water flowed upward"), armed resistance became increasingly unrealistic. Many Vietnamese officials "retired" or claimed either ill health or family responsibilities prevented them from serving in the government. The ultimate way to withdraw from an unacceptable world was suicide.

In the first decade of the twentieth century, Vietnamese began to explore new possibilities for dealing with the French. Phan Boi Chau (1867–1940), founder of the Association for the Modernization of Vietnam in 1904, wanted to learn from the West. In particular, he saw Japan's efforts to modernize as a useful example and suggested that Vietnamese "Travel East." Where Chau was a revolutionary and also a monarchist, Phan Chu Trinh (1872-1926) emphasized the importance of education and non-violent reform. Together, Chau and Trinh helped to set the boundaries of the twentieth-century Vietnamese struggle for national independence and unity.

One major development in the campaign to free Vietnam from French colonial rule was the development of *quoc ngu*, literally "national language," which was a writing system for Vietnamese based on the Roman alphabet. In the twentieth century, particularly after the traditional examination system based on Confucian texts was abolished, *quoc ngu* took the place of Chinese characters as the national writing system. It was used extensively before and after World War I to spread new ideas. It was far easier to learn to read *quoc ngu* than to master the skill of reading material written with Chinese characters, allowing ideas to spread well beyond the elites.

The *quoc ngu* periodicals of the first part of the twentieth century were important sources for new ways of looking at the world. Particularly in the 1930s, the Vietnamese discussed whether old values should be retained or reinterpreted and the extent to which one might live on the basis of new, Western values. It was the beginnings of a long-term effort to, as Neil Jamieson puts it in *Understanding Vietnam*, "reset the social thermostat."

Newspapers, books, and magazines in *quoc ngu* proliferated in the 1930s. Writers using the new system of writing challenged traditional values and wrote to convince others of the correctness of their position. One of the most famous of the novels from the period, *Breaking the Ties* (1935) by Nguyen Tuong Tam (1906–1963), presented a militant kind of individualism. The protagonist, Loan, was a woman, as was the case in many of the novels that examined the conflict between individualism and community. Where some saw her as the personification of the ideal qualities of the new Vietnamese woman, others saw her as aggressive and arrogant.

Jamieson summarizes the main tendency of this period:

> Virtually all literary figures, as well as all political activists, were working to create a new and different world. With one voice they were prepared to condemn both the traditional sociocultural system of Vietnam and the French colonial administration that overlay it. Where they were divided, and with increasing bitterness as time went on, was in deciding how change could best be accomplished, and in defining the nature of the new society that would replace the existing one.
>
> (*Understanding Vietnam*, p. 174)

Political activism among the Vietnamese in the 1920s took two main directions. One, the Vietnam National Party (Viet Nam Quoc Dan Dang or VNQDD), was founded in 1927. A moderate socialist party, it is often credited with being the first revolutionary party in Vietnam. The party achieved considerable success in recruiting members in the late 1920s from teachers, bureaucrats, and non-commissioned officers in the army. In February 1930, under pressure from the French authorities, the VNQDD decided to launch a series of surprise attacks. Although they had a brief success at Yen Bay where they held the town for a day, the French crushed them. Thirteen VNQDD leaders were guillotined, hundreds of others executed, and thousands sentenced to prison. Many fled to China and gained limited support from the Chinese Nationalists.

The second strand eventually became the basis for the Indochinese Communist Party. Ho Chi Minh (1890–1969), then known as Nguyen Ai Quoc (Nguyen the Patriot), in 1925 organized the Vietnam Revolutionary Youth Association (Viet Nam Thanh Nien Cach Mang Dong Chi Hoi), as an organization dedicated to the struggle against imperialism and for social justice. The Revolutionary Youth League combined the ideas of national liberation and land reform and blended a modified Marxism–Leninism with patriotism. One of its most important contributions was the front concept, the idea of making temporary alliances with non-Communists in order to achieve revolutionary goals. It reached out both to the peasantry and to the urban middle classes.

At this point, Quoc (i.e. Ho) was foremost a nationalist. The draft program for the Revolutionary Youth League contained a pledge to struggle to overthrow imperialism and re-establish national independence, and then to turn to participation in the world revolution to work for the end of class distinctions, "the final goal for which we are fighting." Quoc and his associates published several journals. He also wrote a basic Marxist text, *The Revolutionary Path*. Although essentially a Leninist discussion, it emphasized the crucial role of the rural classes in the revolutionary partnership with the proletariat.

In February 1930 Quoc and his associates dealt with the existence of three separate Indochinese communist parties by forming a new party. At first called the Vietnamese Communist Party, it became known as the Indochinese Communist Party (ICP) in October of that year. Quoc's emphasis on national goals was criticized both within and outside the party. In ways quite similar to Mao Zedong in China, and at very nearly the same time, Quoc struggled to get his perspective accepted within the party.

The new party immediately faced a wave of peasant insurrections and worker strikes in Nghe An (Quoc's home province) and Ha Tinh in central Vietnam. Revolutionaries in Nghe An organized a *soviet* or revolutionary council that redistributed land, abolished taxes, and performed other governmental tasks. Although it survived from the spring of 1930 to the middle of 1931, the movement had no real chance. Hundreds were killed and thousands arrested. Many of the future leaders, Vo Nguyen Giap, Le Duan, Pham Van Dong, and Le Duc Tho among them, gained a traditional revolutionary education in the French prisons. Quoc was also arrested by the British in Hong Kong, but released in 1932.

The French seemed solidly in control of Indochina in the 1930s. They also regarded themselves as benefactors of the Vietnamese. Colonial officials put forward the image of "*le colon batisseur*," the colonist who was constructing railroad lines, highways, harbors, mines, rubber plantations, and the many grand buildings in Hanoi and Saigon. While some Vietnamese benefited from the introduction of capitalism and an export-driven economy, most did not. Working conditions, worst on the rubber plantations in the south where virtual slavery prevailed, were also relatively bad in mines and factories. The best new land, created by draining parts of the Mekong Delta in the south, went to the French. Peasants found it difficult to pay the high taxes levied by the French to pay for the improvements they sponsored. The Vietnamese had few opportunities to gain an education and not many employment possibilities if they should become educated. Still, while most Vietnamese despised the French colonial regime, there seemed little chance it could be overthrown and the nation restored.

The August Revolution and the Nine-Year National Resistance, 1945–1954

After the British released Nyugen Ai Quoc from custody in 1932, he went into exile in the Soviet Union until 1938. Returning that year to China, he began to make connections again with the Vietnamese revolutionary movement. In 1940, after the Germans defeated the French, he realized the importance of returning to Indochina. In 1941 he moved to Pac Bo in the northern part of Vietnam. There, at the Eight Plenum of the Indochinese Communist Party in May, he and his associates founded the Vietminh Front (also known as the League for the Independence of Vietnam or Viet Nam Doc Lap Dong Minh Hoi). The emphasis of the Vietminh program was on national liberation from the French colonial regime and the Japanese occupation forces. The program also touched on what it called "antifeudalism" and social change. This, however, was a delicate area in that the Vietminh wanted to attract wide support. The Vietminh wanted to appeal not only to landless laborers and poor peasants but also to the better-off peasants and even to "patriotic landlords." Then, too, they wanted to enlist the nationalistic middle classes and the intelligentsia. Too much emphasis on social justice would cost them the support of those whose chief aim was national liberation. Policies that had been criticized in the early 1930s were now accepted and Ho Chi Minh, "Ho the Bringer of Light," as he had begun to call himself, emerged as the leading figure in the Vietminh.

The Vietminh in the next few years followed the lead of the Chinese Communists. Cadres, for example, were required to help the peasantry, pay attention to local customs, learn the local languages, and to buy or borrow only what people wanted to sell or lend. The Vietminh made a concerted effort to establish good relations with the many minority people in the area. They also established a working relationship with American OSS agents (Office of Strategic Services – the forerunner of the CIA) by providing some military intelligence and helping to rescue downed American pilots. In return, the OSS provided supplies and equipment. Ho possibly also hoped for American support against the return of the French when the time came.

The Japanese coup against the French in March 1945 was far more important than American aid, however. This attack disabled the colonial regime and created a space for the Vietminh. The Japanese, far more worried about the possibility of an allied invasion of Indochina than about Vietnamese nationalist movements, did not pay the same kind of attention to the Vietminh the French had. The Vietminh also gained support by their attempts to deal with the widespread famine in the north. Although there were limits to what they could do, it was far more than the Japanese, who controlled the food supplies, were willing to do.

What the Vietnamese call the August Revolution resembled the October Revolution in Russia in some important ways. It was, first, an audacious move. No other group tried or was prepared to move into the political space created by the Japanese surrender. It was also a move centered on a single, charismatic figure, Ho Chi Minh. However, where Russia in 1917 had been in a state of near-anarchy and external forces prevented from intervening by the continuation of World War I, the colonial regime in Indochina was only temporarily disabled and World War II ended just as the Vietminh were seizing power.

On 2 September 1945 Ho Chi Minh and the Vietminh celebrated Vietnamese independence in a massive gathering at Ba Dinh Square in Hanoi (today the site of Ho's mausoleum). Ho began with quotations from the American Declaration of Independence and the French Declaration of the Rights of Man and Citizen. He contrasted the ideals expressed by these two documents with French colonial practices. Ho attempted to tap into the substantial revolutionary tradition and the large body of radical political thought that existed by the middle of the twentieth century. The French and American Revolutions had generated important universal ideas about citizenship, representative politics, and equality before the law that supposedly were applicable anywhere in the world. Ho's efforts to appeal to the revolutionary heritage of France and also the United States fell on deaf ears, however. The national interests of these countries trumped any reference to revolutionary origins.

Ho concluded his talk by noting that:

> [W]e, members of the Provisional Government of the Democratic Republic of Vietnam, solemnly declare to the world that Vietnam has the right to be a free and independent country – it is so already. The entire Vietnamese people are determined to mobilize all their physical and mental strength, to sacrifice their lives and property, in order to safeguard their independence and liberty.

The celebration over, the Democratic Republic of Vietnam (DRV) began to face reality. In the south, reality was the British, who had come to receive the surrender of the Japanese. They decided to re-arm the French, and assist them in a coup against the Vietminh Executive Committee that had been administering Saigon. In the north, the DRV had to contend with the Chinese Nationalist forces that had come to carry out the surrender and disarming of Japanese forces in that area.

In February 1946, the Chinese signed a treaty with the French and withdrew. This left the Vietminh alone with the French. Ho negotiated an agreement on 6 March 1946 with the French negotiator, Jean Sainteny, avoiding bloodshed, but only for the time being as it turned out. French troops could land in the north. They would withdraw later, leaving Vietnam free of foreign soldiers by 1952. Vietnam would be a "free state" within an Indochinese Federation of the French Union. It was a compromise solution that might have worked had the French been willing to carry it out. Instead, Ho negotiated fruitlessly in France during the summer of 1946, obtaining only an agreement that largely repeated the agreement of 6 March.

The tense situation came to a head in November. The French bombarded the port city of Haiphong, killing several thousand Vietnamese. Ho continued to negotiate for nearly a month, but on 19 December 1946, the Nine-Year National Resistance (the Indochina War) began. An undeclared war in the south had already begun in 1945. And, although there would be a lull after 1954, the war became a "Thirty Year War," as Marilyn B. Young has labeled it in *The Vietnam Wars, 1945–1990*.

If Ho, as the "Lenin" of Vietnam, had been primarily responsible for the August Revolution and the establishment of the Democratic Republic of Vietnam, Vo Nguyen Giap (1911–) was the Trotsky of Vietnam, the organizer of the People's Army of Vietnam (PAVN) and the brilliant strategist of the Indochina War. In 1944 Giap put together an Armed Propaganda Team (APT). By the time of the August Revolution he commanded a few thousand troops, basically a guerrilla army. At the start of the war, the army was somewhat bigger but still badly equipped.

The French controlled a large part of Cochin China in the south, the Red River Delta in the north, and the major cities. The Vietminh controlled much of the countryside, especially in the north. Although the French were determined to hold Indochina, they could not commit the necessary manpower and matériel to do so. Because of French domestic politics, it was not possible to use draftees, which limited the French to professional soldiers and Vietnamese troops. Until the United States began giving the French massive amounts of aid, the war effort was hampered by the needs of reconstruction in metropolitan France. Finally, the French used, almost exclusively, military means to gain their objectives. Even when they attempted to win over Vietnamese nationalists by establishing a State of Vietnam under Emperor Bao Dai, it was clear that the state was not sovereign. The contest raged on between Vietnamese nationalists, many of who were Marxists, and what most Vietnamese regarded as a brutal French colonial regime.

Two external events changed the nature of the conflict. First, the victory of the Chinese Communists in 1949 led to recognition of the DRV and, more important, to large amounts of supplies and equipment coming across the borders between China and Vietnam. Secondly, the United States, even before the Korean War began, began to provide the French with aid. French support for American policy in Europe was considered crucial. After 1949, and especially once the Korean War began, the US supported the French in Indochina as part of the worldwide struggle against Communism. At the end, it was paying most of the costs of the war. US aid, although sizeable, was not enough. According to some commentators, the war was lost by 1950 when Giap's forces won control of a highway (known as RC4) that ran parallel to the Chinese border.

In 1951 Giap shifted to a conventional style of warfare. Although he was not successful and had to return to a guerrilla-style campaign, the Vietnamese learned a great deal about dealing with French tactics and weapons. In the campaigns over the next two years, neither side was able to gain a decisive advantage.

Giap's invasion of Laos in 1953 drew a response from the French, the establishment of a base in the northwest of Vietnam that blocked the Vietminh invasion route into Laos. The French commander, General Henri Navarre, hoped either to block the Vietminh invasion or to draw the Vietminh forces into a conventional battle in which French artillery and air power would destroy them.

The site selected was Dien Bien Phu, a village set in a large valley. The French conceded the high ground around the valley to the Vietminh. The siege took place between 13 March and 7 May. The key factor was Giap's ability to get artillery supplied by the Chinese to the high ground surrounding the valley. The French journalist Bernard Fall, who wrote about the siege in *Hell in a Very Small Place*, noted Giap's artillery created an impossible situation for the French defenders. The inadequacy of French air support was another factor.

Leaders in Washington, DC discussed the possibility of an American intervention. A few even broached the idea of using atom bombs. Ironically, Lyndon Baines Johnson was one of those who spoke out forcefully against the use of American forces to aid the French.

What the Vietminh gained on the battlefield, they lost at the conference table. At the Geneva Conference, the Soviet Union and the People's Republic of China (PRC) pressed the DRV to accept a compromise agreement. The Geneva Accords recognized the independence of Cambodia, Laos, and Vietnam. The latter was temporarily divided pending unification at the 17th parallel. Troops were required to regroup; civilians could do likewise if they wished. National elections to determine the new government for all of Vietnam were to take place in two years. The accords also forbade Vietnam, Laos, and Cambodia from participating in military alliances.

The DRV reluctantly bowed to Russian and Chinese pressure and accepted the agreement. This probably reflected Ho's characteristic willingness to negotiate and compromise without, however, giving up ultimate goals. The Soviet Union and the PRC plainly hoped to ease Cold War tensions and were not above sacrificing some of the interests of the Vietnamese in the process. The United States was not happy with the accords. It pledged not to use force or the threat of force to undermine the accords, but it seems clear the United States intended to block unification, which most observers thought would result in a communist Vietnam.

The two Vietnams and the United States, 1954–1975

The crucial figure in the State of Vietnam (South Vietnam) was not the Emperor Bao Dai but the man he appointed prime minister, Ngo Dinh Diem (1901–1963). Diem, from an old Mandarin family in Vietnam, had good connections with American politicians. Diem's main power bases were Vietnamese Catholics, including about a million that had moved south from the DRV, the landed gentry, and anti-communist nationalists. Most nationalists, however, did not support him. Nor did the powerful religious sects, the Cao Dai and the Hoa Hao.

Without American support, it seems doubtful that Diem would have survived. By 1956, the United States had pressured the French to leave, encouraged Diem not to proceed with Vietnam-wide elections, and managed to extend the protection of the Southeast Asia Treaty Organization (SEATO) to Vietnam. It had also supported Diem in the referendum in 1955 between Bao Dai and Diem. On the basis of the referendum, the results of which were falsified, Diem proclaimed the Republic of Vietnam (RVN) with himself as president. Also in 1955 Diem defeated the Binh Xuyen, a powerful criminal organization, and weakened the power of the religious sects.

Diem resisted American efforts to turn him into an American-style politician who would at least go through the motions of land reform and attend to the need for education, public health, and community development for the majority of the population. Most of the American aid went toward the military or was used in the cities, where only a minority of the population lived.

In the remainder of the 1950s Diem instituted authoritarian rule, appointing Catholics in key positions and people loyal to him in other posts. Members of his family possessed great power, especially his brother, Ngo Dinh Nhu, whom he appointed head of the secret police. The National Legislative Assembly was largely a façade. Diem also arrested hundreds of Vietminh who had remained in the south to work in the planned elections. By 1960 opposition was growing in the south. Representatives of the opposition in the south met in December 1960 to form the National Liberation Front (NLF). This event, as delegates to the meeting that founded the NLF recognized, marked the beginning of a new era in the two Vietnams.

During the mid-1950s, the DVR had its first opportunity to use the power it had gained in the war against the French. Heavily influenced by the practices of the Chinese Communists, the government sponsored a land reform movement. Prepared in 1952 and 1953 and begun in 1955, this movement quickly gained a momentum of its own. As is often the case in movements of this sort, old scores were settled and some took advantage of the situation to advance the interests of their families. A growing paranoia ensured that many innocent people were deprived of land and were, in some cases, executed. The bitterness this caused in the villages led the Lao Dong (Workers) Party (founded in 1951) to criticize the movement and to try to rectify mistakes. The campaign was relatively moderate compared to a similar campaign in the PRC. One historian estimates that anywhere from 3,000 to 15,000 people were executed. Other estimates are far higher, but are often politically motivated. Large numbers also died of hunger or disease.

The process by which cooperatives and, later, collective farms were established was slower and more carefully prepared. By 1960 some 86 percent of the rural population was in a village cooperative of some sort. Eight years later 90 percent belonged to collectives. On the whole, land reform in its broadest sense, together with the rectification campaign, resulted in a government that was still popular and respected in the 1960s. The interests of the collective outweighed the needs of the individual. The traditional idea of imposing constraints on individual behavior echoed basic teachings of Vietnamese tradition.

Industrialization, however, did not make much headway in the 1950s. In 1961 a Five-Year Plan for the rapid development of heavy industry was put in place. Soviet aid up to that point had been crucial to the development of the DRV. Surprisingly, it had come close to matching American aid to the south. However, each nation used its power, money, and material aid in very different ways.

As early as 1956, responding to Diem's campaign to eliminate Vietminh cadre and his refusal to cooperate in holding nationwide elections, party members in the north began to discuss ways in which they might move from political to military measures. Taking the lead in this was Le Duan (1907–1986), head of the Regional Committee of the South. In 1957 the government launched an assassination campaign in the south and also organized armed groups. In January 1959 the party decided to use armed force to topple the Diem Government. At the Third Congress of the Lao Dong Party in September 1960, Le Duan was named as secretary-general. The two tasks of revolution were (1) to "carry out the socialist revolution in the north" and (2) to "achieve national unification."

Shortly after the Third Congress of the Lao Dong Party, in December 1960 delegates from the nationalist opposition met to form the NLF. The Lao Dong Party created the Central Office for South Vietnam (COSVN) to serve as a liaison between it and the NLF. The question remains to what extent the NLF was an autonomous entity. It appeared to be, and was to some extent, an independent and spontaneous revolutionary movement. As such, it gained worldwide support and sympathy. It was, however, increasingly dependent on the DVR for aid and support.

In the new era, the scale of conflict involving the two Vietnams and the United States escalated rapidly, culminating in the bloody year of 1968. None of the principal players foresaw or intended the consequences that flowed from the actions they took in this period.

In 1963 the situation in South Vietnam reached a point of crisis. Buddhist protests against a ban on flying their flag led to the killing of nine demonstrators by riot police in May. The following month, Thich Quang Duc, a Buddhist monk, set himself on fire in protest. In the meantime, the United States, through its ambassador, Henry Cabot Lodge, assured South Vietnamese generals of American support for a coup. In the coup that began on 1 November 1963, both Diem and his brother were killed.

A period of political instability followed the coup. While it is difficult to characterize public opinion in South Vietnam, there are indications that many Vietnamese hoped for a neutral and also non-communist South Vietnam. They recognized the dangers of a confrontation between an anti-communist government backed by the United States and the NLF backed by the DRV. They feared war would bring massive destruction and loss of life to the country. Other Vietnamese appeared to think that South Vietnam could remain non-communist only with the assistance of the United States. Nguyen Van Thieu (1923–2001), elected president in September 1967, at last brought back political stability to South Vietnam through authoritarian rule. He loudly proclaimed his willingness to cooperate with the United States.

In the meantime, the United States had moved from an advisory role under President John F. Kennedy to an interventionist role under President Lyndon Baines Johnson. The military and foreign policy advisors for the two presidents were largely the same. Most were convinced that the United States, as the most powerful nation in the postwar world, had the military, economic, and technological capacity to defeat a Third World revolutionary movement. It was a clear case of hubris, the inability of "The Best and the Brightest," as David Halberstam put it in the title of his book, to recognize the constraints imposed by the situation in South Vietnam.

First and foremost, the struggle in South Vietnam was being played out within the context of the Cold War. It was on one level a proxy war, at least until the United States intervened directly. Since the Soviet Union and the PRC supported the DRV, the United States could only go so far in the steps it might take against the DRV without risking a widening of the war, which limited available military options.

On another level, the struggle in South Vietnam was a civil war and a war for "hearts and minds." It was not likely to be won through the use of conventional military power. The extraordinary mobility and firepower of the United States only went so far against an enemy that used mostly guerrilla tactics.

Operating against the US efforts, even those concerned with winning hearts and minds, were the endemic corruption and opportunism that massive US intervention fostered in Vietnam. It is deeply ironic that the infusion of capital and goods from the United States in the mid-1960s began to erode the value system and the culture of South Vietnam. In an era of rapidly rising prices, high-ranking military officers and government officials found their salaries completely inadequate. Bar girls or people with access to the cornucopia of American products flourished. In addition, military sweeps produced thousands of refugees. Bombing and defoliation campaigns (Agent Orange) changed the landscape. In the process of attempting to save South Vietnam from Communism, the United States was creating a very different country. It was, in some respects, a revolution within the revolution, and one with particularly unattractive outcomes.

The Gulf of Tonkin incident took place in August 1964. This involved a brief skirmish in North Vietnamese territorial waters between North Vietnamese torpedo boats and an American destroyer. A possible second attack occurred two days later (the evidence is inconclusive and it is likely there was no second attack). The congressional resolution that followed what the administration assumed was a second attack gave President Johnson carte blanche to deal with the situation in Vietnam. The following year the United States sent large numbers of American combat troops into South Vietnam. Two years later about half a million American soldiers were carrying out most of the efforts to deal with the NLF. At the same time, a sizeable movement protesting against the war began to take shape in the United States.

By the end of 1967 the Vietnamese Revolution, from the perspective of the DRV and the NLF, had begun to take on a very different shape from the Nine-Year National Resistance against the French. To some extent, of course, the image of the Vietminh had always been somewhat romanticized. While most were dedicated and did their best to adhere to the ideas about how they should treat the peasants they worked among, coercion, intimidation, and simply bad behavior sometimes took place. The NLF tried to live up to the example of the Vietminh, but found it much more difficult to operate in South Vietnam. The close-knit village structure characteristic of the north was often missing in the south, where many peasants were landless laborers. Villagers were, in any case, generally caught between what the NLF (or the Viet Cong as their opponents labeled them) wanted them to do and what the South Vietnamese and Americans wanted. Coercion, intimidation, and assassination were much more in evidence in what the NLF and the DRV called the American War. The NLF also depended on supplies and on North Vietnamese regular troops sent south from the DRV along the Ho Chi Minh Trail. Finally, the Vietnamese Revolution had by 1968 become much more of a military operation than an effort to persuade the peasantry of the virtues of revolution, whether for national unity or for social justice.

The Tet Offensive in 1968 marked a new phase in the revolution. Tet is the holiday marking the beginning of the lunar New Year in Vietnam and it is also the most important holiday in the Vietnamese calendar. The DRV and the NLF chose this time to launch a massive attack on the major cities and towns in South Vietnam. For the first time, they carried the war into urban areas. One hope was to galvanize the revolution and provoke a popular uprising. Another was to achieve stunning military victories that would convince the United States it was not possible to defeat the NLF and DRV. If they could do this, the United States might decide to negotiate.

Militarily, the campaign resulted in defeat for the DRV and the NLF. They were unable to hold the positions they had taken. The NLF in particular lost heavily in terms of personnel and probably also in terms of influence. Increasingly in the next few years, soldiers and officials from the north dominated the revolution in the south. This had important repercussions when victory came in 1975. Cadre in the south did not necessarily want the same kinds of political and socio-economic arrangements as those in the north, but they found themselves overwhelmed in the movement toward unification.

Tet had a great impact on American opinion about the war. Brutal images, such as that of the Saigon police chief summarily executing a suspected VC by shooting him in the head or television reports of the fierce fighting in Hue, convinced many Americans that the war might not be winnable. Since they had only shortly before been told that it was possible to see the light at the end of the tunnel, a massive "credibility gap" opened up. How much had they not been told? Advisors to President Johnson now counseled him to find a way to extricate the United States from the war.

The Vietnamese Revolution played a large role in creating what seemed to some Americans to be a revolutionary situation in the United States in 1968. Other factors included the turn to Black Power in the Civil Rights Movement, student rebellions on many campuses, a growing (if diffuse) counterculture, and the assassination first of Martin Luther King, Jr., and then of Robert Kennedy in the course of 1968.

There was little danger of revolution in the United States in 1968, however, despite the ideas cherished by some members of the Students for Democratic Society (SDS) and the Youth International Party (Yippies). Nonetheless, it was time of considerable turmoil and questioning of American values and institutions. It was, in many ways, an attempt to deal with unfinished business from the American Revolution. Domestically, Reverend King had pointed out ways in which American blacks had not been allowed to participate fully in the American Dream. Abroad, the United States appeared to be denying the Vietnamese the very goals that·had been a central part of the American Revolution: self-government and freedom from foreign rule.

Richard M. Nixon (1913–1994) won the presidential race in 1968, at least in part because he claimed to have a plan for ending the war. He actually had no plan, but he did develop a two-pronged strategy. One part of the strategy called for the *Vietnamization* of the war. The South Vietnamese military was enlarged and equipped so that it could fight the war largely on its own. Americans, however, would continue to provide airpower and supply the South Vietnamese with weaponry. A second part emphasized negotiation, but negotiation from strength. President Nixon, like President Johnson before him, did not want to sign a treaty that acknowledged defeat in the war. The treaty finally signed in 1973 was much the same treaty that could have been signed in 1969. Thousands of Americans and hundreds of thousands of Vietnamese had died in the meantime, mainly because Nixon and his chief foreign policy advisor, Henry Kissinger, sought to force North Vietnam to accept their terms.

In his efforts to put pressure on the North Vietnamese and the NLF, President Nixon authorized a move that had fateful consequences for Cambodia. In 1970, in an effort to find COSVN, the headquarters of the revolutionary movement in the south, the United States staged an "incursion" into Cambodia. This, together with the American bombing campaigns, destabilized Cambodian politics and led to the takeover in 1975 by Pol Pot (1928–1998) and the Khmer Rouge (Cambodian communists). In the new state of Kampuchea, Pol Pot's utopian agrarian policies caused the deaths of perhaps as many as two million Cambodians, a quarter of the population. The use of revolutionary power in the case of Kampuchea devastated the country.

President Nixon had promised President Thieu that US forces would come to the aid of South Vietnam if North Vietnam attacked in strength. However, the controversy over the attempts to cover up the Watergate burglary led to President Nixon's resignation in 1974. By this time, Congress had already passed the War Powers Act, greatly restricting presidential powers. When the North Vietnamese invaded the Central Highlands in 1975, the United States did not come to President Thieu's aid as Nixon had promised. The South Vietnamese response to the invasion turned an organized retreat into a rout. South Vietnam surrendered on 30 April 1975.

Conclusion

In the more than twenty-five years since the unification of Vietnam in 1975 and the creation of the new Socialist Republic of Vietnam (SRV) in 1976, the Vietnamese Revolution has yet to find its way. In 1976 the Fourth Party Congress met for the first time since 1960. It changed the name of the Lao Dong Party to that of the Vietnamese Communist Party and decreed the need to develop socialism throughout the SRV.

The major immediate task was to knit together the two very different areas of the country. The government followed standard communist policies emphasizing heavy industry and collectivization of agriculture with a singular lack of success. It also became involved in military ventures, achieving in the 1978 invasion and occupation of Cambodia a limited success in that it ended genocide in that country. Despite that fact Vietnam became something of an international pariah.

In the 1980s, Vietnam, maintaining the world's fourth largest armed forces and a bloated government bureaucracy, approached economic collapse. In 1985 famine and inflation of 400 to 600 percent pushed Vietnam to the edge. The following year, at the Sixth National Communist Party Congress, the leadership announced a series of changes that created space for a limited return of free enterprise. Many of the hardliners from the 1960s and 1970s had either died (Le Duan) or retired (Pham Van Dong, Le Duc Tho, and Truong Chinh).

Nguyen Van Linh, the new party secretary, introduced a reform program known as *doi moi* (renovation).

Over the next decade economic reforms produced positive but also uneven results. The party remained divided between conservatives and those more liberal. The events of 1989 in Eastern Europe in particular raised fears that the party might lose control of the country politically. In the 1990s foreign investments in the billions poured into Vietnamese and jointly owned enterprises. The economy averaged 8 percent growth a year. Yet the party with its aging leadership and bloated bureaucracy remained the major obstacle to growth and change. At the end of the century, with the Asian economic miracle in tatters, Vietnam, a would-be Asian tiger, remained a poor country under an authoritarian government, the memories of revolutionary dedication and sacrifice largely meaningless to the millions of Vietnamese born after 1975.

The memory of the heroic struggles, first against the French, then against the Americans, is the major legacy of the Vietnamese Revolution. For thirty years, off and on, a poor nation with little industry struggled to win its independence and to unify the country. Under Ho Chi Minh, the Vietminh proved masters at motivating the peasantry, the relatively small working class, and many from the middle classes and intelligentsia to sacrifice for the nation. The fact that Vietnam had a long history, a good part of which had been taken up with the struggle for independence from China, assisted the Vietminh in establishing a broad and powerful movement. The French assisted in their own way by seeking military solutions and failing to reform colonial practices or to offer the prospect of genuine independence. Non-communist nationalists found it difficult to overcome partisan politics and almost impossible to offer the lower classes reasons to follow them.

In the 1950s and 1960s, after the division of Vietnam in 1954, Ho's influence began to wane. Chinese ideas about land reform and a powerful Marxist party gained prominence. While the NLF was often successful in using the tactics of the Vietminh and the Chinese Communist guerrillas against the South Vietnamese and then against the Americans, the revolution in the south quickly turned into the American War. Supplies and soldiers coming from the DRV down the Ho Chi Minh Trail became essential. The DRV developed into a nation in arms, in a small way replicating the experience of the French Revolution, but it was not able to overcome the massive military power of the United States. The latter, for its part, under the influence of Cold War rhetoric and believing in various myths about the bloodbaths that would follow a communist victory, failed to notice how it was destroying the very country it had meant to save. The famous line uttered by a US army officer in 1968 comes to mind: "We had to destroy the town in order to save it."

The victors in the Vietnamese Revolution had achieved an extraordinary success in their heroic struggle to unify the country. They had, however, only stale, long-outmoded ideas about what to do with power once it had been gained. The Marxist revolutionary ideas available in the mid-1970s, whether

Soviet or Chinese, were not working for the countries from which they came, and were not relevant to the needs of a devastated, extremely poor country trying to recover from decades of nearly continuous war. Ho's commitment to a combination of moderate and pragmatic Marxism and nationalism was no longer available. General Giap, although still influential, had been eclipsed by other party figures and chose inexplicably to remain largely above the fray.

The intriguing possibility of working with its erstwhile rival, the United States, faded by the end of the 1970s. The Vietnamese invasion of Cambodia ended whatever chances there might have been of American and World Bank funds for reconstruction. It would have been no small irony, of course, to fight for revolutionary victory for years on end, only to surrender to enemy ideas about the economy and society once victory had been won. Perhaps, however, in the end, something like that occurred. Observers note the growing differences between the south, where capitalism seems to have taken hold again, and the north.

Revolutionary romanticism stripped away, Vietnam and its revolution form one of the great historical tragedies of the twentieth century. If revolution is politics by another means, it is difficult not to think that statesmen on both sides should have had the wisdom to see the need to move back to conventional politics at some point in the 1950s. Of course, in the paranoid atmosphere created by events of the Cold War, such a cool and rational judgment could hardly have been expected. As with revolutions before the Vietnamese Revolution and after it, history produced it and in turn it shaped history.

Further reading

Buttinger, Joseph (1958) *The Smaller Dragon: A Political History of Vietnam*. New York: Praeger.

Duiker, William J. (1976) *The Rise of Nationalism in Vietnam, 1900–1941*. Ithaca, NY: Cornell University Press.

—— (2000) *Ho Chi Minh*. New York: Hyperion.

Elliott, Duong Van Mai (1999) *The Sacred Willow: Four Generations in the Life of a Vietnamese Family*. New York: Oxford University Press.

Fall, Bernard (1967) *Hell in a Very Small Place: The Siege of Dien Bien Phu*. Philadelphia: Lippincott.

Gardner, Lloyd C. (1995) *Pay any Price: Lyndon Johnson and the Wars for Vietnam*. Chicago: I. R. Dee.

Gilbert, Marc Jason (editor) (2002) *Why North Vietnam Won the War*. New York: Palgrave.

Halberstam, David (1972) *The Best and the Brightest*. New York: Random House.

Herring, George C. (1996) *America's Longest War: The United States and Vietnam, 1950–1975*, third edition. New York: McGraw-Hill.

Jamieson, Neil (1993) *Understanding Vietnam*. Berkeley: University of California Press.

Kaiser, David (2000) *American Tragedy: Kennedy, Johnson, and the Origins of the Vietnam War*. Cambridge, MA: Harvard University Press.

Khanh, Huynh Kim (1982) *Vietnamese Communism, 1925–1945*. Ithaca, NY: Cornell University Press.

Marr, David (1971) *Vietnamese Anti-Colonialism, 1885–1925*. Berkeley: University of California Press.

—— (1981) *Vietnamese Tradition on Trial, 1920–1945*. Berkeley: University of California Press.

—— (1995) *Vietnam 1945. The Quest for Power*. Berkeley: University of California Press.

Moise, Edwin E. (1983) *Land Reform in China and North Vietnam: Consolidating the Revolution at the Village Level*. Chapel Hill: University of North Carolina Press.

Thayer, Carlyle (1989) *War by Other Means: National Liberation and Revolution in Viet-Nam 1954–1960*. Sydney: Allen & Unwin.

Tonnesson, Stein (1991) *The Vietnamese Revolution of 1945: Roosevelt, Ho Chi Minh, and de Gaulle in a World at War*. London: Sage.

Tucker, Spencer C. (editor) (1998) *The Encyclopedia of the Vietnam War: A Political, Social, and Military History*. Oxford and New York: Oxford University Press.

Young, Marilyn B. (1991) *The Vietnam Wars, 1945–1990*. New York: Harper Collins.

Chapter 6

The Iranian Revolution

Religion has played a role in each of the revolutions examined in this book. It was generally the victim of the policies instituted by the new revolutionary regimes. The Iranian Revolution presents a different case, one in which religion was not simply a factor but the major factor. Even more than the British Revolution in the middle of the seventeenth century, religion became the defining issue. However, quite unlike the case of the British Revolution, religion in Iran shaped the revolution and dominated the regime that emerged from the revolutionary experience. Islamic fundamentalism continues to play a paramount role in Iranian life more than two decades after the revolutionaries came to power. It is not yet possible to see precisely what the impact of Islamic fundamentalism will be in Iran in the long term.

The Iranian Revolution, however, is concerned with more than just Islamic fundamentalism. It offers a case study in the difficulties of bringing about rapid change in economic, social, and cultural matters while maintaining an authoritarian political system. Modernization in the different sectors of Iranian life, political, economic, social, and cultural, led to vocal opposition by groups that opposed the new arrangements. Many Iranians welcomed urbanization, secularization, economic change, and opportunities for social mobility. Others, particularly the Islamic clergy and the *bazaaris*, the merchants and shopkeepers from the older sector of the middle class, did not want to see the traditional way of life disappear. In many respects, Iran repeated the patterns first experienced by Mexico and Russia, where government sponsored attempts to keep pace with Western Europe and the United States created problems and instabilities.

The Cold War context was also a major factor in the Iranian Revolution, although in ways different from its impact in Vietnam. Politics in Iran from the 1940s on were shaped by the contest between the Soviet Union and the United States. The United States strongly influenced the course of Iranian history beginning in the early 1950s and inadvertently did much to bring on the revolution and the Islamic fundamentalist regime that it produced.

Is the Iranian Revolution a departure from a tradition that goes back to the French Revolution (and even to the British Revolution of the seventeenth century), a tradition taken up and transformed by the Russian experience? Is it perhaps merely an idiosyncratic product of economic, political, social, and cultural forces at work in the twentieth century, a local phenomenon that did not follow the models presented by the French and Russian Revolutions? Or perhaps it is more than a local phenomenon, the harbinger of a wave of revolutions based solidly on the foundations of Islamic fundamentalism. It does, in its own way, aspire to a utopian system, offering a seamless web of politics, economics, and culture, but the system is meant to preserve or revive much of the past rather than install something new and innovative. Nonetheless, one of the dynamic pressures that continue to operate in the Iranian Revolution is the desire on the part of many of the poor, both in the countryside and in the cities, to deal with social and economic issues. And, as has become apparent in recent years, there remains a strong interest in democratic and representative government, informed perhaps but not dominated by religious teachings.

The Constitutional Revolution (1906)

Persia (as Iran was then known) experienced a revolution that introduced constitutionalism and democracy at about the same time as similar developments occurred in China, Mexico, Russia, and the Ottoman Empire. The revolution was a product of nationalistic reactions to the influence of other countries, in this case, Britain and Russia; damage to local commercial interests caused by the operations of the modern world economy; and interest in modern political ideas such as democratic elections, parliaments, and constitutions.

Early in the twentieth century, a coalition formed that included politicians interested in constitutional monarchy; merchants, shopkeepers, and guilds worried about economic change and foreign competition; and the *ulama*, or clerical establishment, and theology students concerned about social and cultural change. The Russian Revolution of 1905 acted as an external catalyst.

In the course of 1905 nationalists combined with leading clerics to sponsor protests against government policies that, while designed to increase revenue, also opened the country to foreign imports. By the middle of 1906 several thousand protesters had sought sanctuary in the gardens of the British Legation in Tehran. Leading reformers formed a committee to discuss the idea of constitutional government with those who had taken sanctuary. Strikes in the city increased the pressure on reformers and the government alike. Giving in to the pressure, Muzaffar al-Din Shah agreed in August 1906 to the formation of a National Consultative *Majles* or parliament.

Despite successful efforts by the government to limit the franchise in the electoral laws of September 1906 a somewhat radical *majles* was elected. The electoral laws excluded women from voting; property and language restrictions also kept many men from voting. The franchise was limited to the *ulama* and theology students, nobles, landowners and small-holders, and merchants and guild members. The large number of representatives from guilds and from the cities of Tabriz and Tehran actually created a more radical *majles* than would have been the case with universal suffrage.

The constitution of December 1906 gave deputies extensive power of the purse, including the right to ratify major financial transactions and to ban foreign loans. It also limited the authority of the shah and his ministers and curtailed foreign influence. Social democrats, influenced by the Russian experience, joined with liberals in establishing a free press and secular judicial codes.

The new monarch, Muhammad 'Ali Shah (ruled 1907–1909) was encouraged by conservative clerics and landowners to challenge the *majles*. In the struggle that ensued, the Supplementary Constitutional Law of 1907 provided a compromise but it was one that ultimately favored the conservatives. While Persian males were granted equal rights, all rights had to conform to *shari'a* (religious laws). The *ulama*, some of who had supported the revolution originally, gained unprecedented power through a council of clerics that had authority over the *majles*. Although the council did not function in the constitutional period, it set a precedent for the future.

In 1908 the shah disbanded the first *majles*. The revolutionary center moved to Tabriz, a city in the northwest. In 1909 the revolutionary army that formed there, known as the *mujahidin*, conquered Tehran. Muhammad 'Ali Shah was deposed and his young son Ahmad Shah (ruled 1909–1925) named shah in his place. Cooperation between the Democrat Party (actually social democratic) and the more conservative Moderate Party gave way to political assassinations, forcible disarmament of most of the *mujahidin*, and exile of prominent social democrats. Under increased pressure from Britain and Russia to get governmental finances in order, the government hired an American, Morgan Shuster, in November 1911 to reorganize the national treasury. The Russian government, however, pressed the Iranian government to dismiss Shuster. Since the British backed the Russian ultimatum and the Russians had dispatched troops in the direction of Tehran, the government had little choice but to dismiss the *majles* in December 1911. This ended Persia's experiment in constitutional government.

The Pahlavi dynasty

After the Bolsheviks came to power in Russia, the British worried about the ability of the Qajar dynasty to keep Communism from Persia. They supported Colonel Reza Khan, commander of the Cossack Brigade (which they now advised). In 1921, Reza Khan used the brigade to stage a virtual coup in which he forced the resignation of the prime minister, taking over the post of minister of war himself. In 1925, after he had expanded the army to 40,000 men, he convinced parliament to vote to depose the Qajar dynasty. Reza Khan adopted the name Pahlavi as the name for his dynasty and became shah-en-shah (king of kings) in 1926.

For more than a decade, Reza Shah Pahlavi worked to modernize Persia (which he renamed Iran ("land of the Aryans") in 1934. He reduced the power of the Shi'i clergy. By simultaneously carrying out popular economic reforms and pro-nationalist policies, he managed to maintain his popularity. He also created a power base in the army and the police and through an extensive patronage system.

By 1941, after the German invasion of the Soviet Union, both Britain and the Soviet Union no longer believed they could trust Reza Shah. In August of that year the Soviet Union occupied northern Iran and the British moved into the south. Reza Shah abdicated in favor of his son, Mohammad Reza, then only twenty years old. This was acceptable to the British who did not wish to destabilize Iran and feared the possibility of increased Russian influence in any case.

Mohammad Reza lacked the charisma and strength that had made his father a successful autocratic leader. It was only in the context of the Cold War and with American support that he became in the 1960s and 1970s the autocratic ruler of Iran and sponsor of the so-called White Revolution.

In 1951 Mohammad Mosaddeq, head of the National Front, an alliance of nationalists, became prime minister. Mosaddeq carried out a reform program that, among other actions, nationalized the Anglo-Iranian Oil Company. The United States and Great Britain responded by organizing a coup in August 1953 meant to restore the shah to full power. Kermit Roosevelt, a son of Theodore Roosevelt, led the American part of the effort.

The coup failed and the shah fled the country. Mosaddeq ordered the army to end the rioting that followed the failure of the coup. This provided an opportunity for General Fazlollah Zahedi to re-launch the coup in the name of restoring order. Pro-Mosaddeq demonstrators were repressed while pro-shah demonstrators, which included anti-communist clerics and pro-shah merchants, joined with pro-shah military units.

The coup led to a number of changes in Iran. First, the shah emerged as a far more powerful figure. Secondly, the United States replaced Great Britain as the major foreign influence in Iranian affairs. Linkage with the United States was both an advantage and a disadvantage for the shah. The United States supplied massive amounts of military equipment over the next twenty-five years and fully supported the shah's efforts over that period to change Iran's economy and society. For many Iranian nationalists and intellectuals, however, the shah could only be seen as "America's shah."

Over the next two decades, the shah worked to change Iran through a combination of reform and repression. For example, General Zahedi, who replaced Mosaddeq as prime minister, launched a campaign of terror in which thousands were arrested and hundreds killed. And, in 1957, the shah, with American support, created SAVAK (Organization of National Security and Intelligence), a secret police agency that quickly gained a reputation for the use of torture.

In the early 1960s the shah announced the White Revolution. One prominent feature was the distribution of land to landless peasants, supposedly as a means of preventing peasant revolution. As was the case with land redistribution in Mexico, Iran's effort did not satisfy the peasantry and created problems not only with the landed upper class but also with the *ulama*. The *ulama* were also landowners and administrators by virtue of some forty thousand charitable religious endowments. This was the beginning of a process by which the shah alienated powerful traditional groups in Iran while failing to offer sufficient incentives to other groups, some of which he helped to bring into being, to support his regime. As in so many other situations, the autocratic leader, increasingly sure of his impregnable position, began to neglect the hard work of maintaining an adequate coalition of support among the powerful and influential.

The White Revolution marked the beginnings of the opposition of Ayatollah Ruhollah Mussavi Khomeini to the shah's regime (Ayatollah is a title carried by only a few clerics in Shi'i Islam; such an individual has the right to make judgments on issues because of his piety and expertise in Islamic law). Ayatollah Khomeini viewed the White Revolution as a movement directed against Islam. His arrest in 1963 led to the June Uprising. Police killed and injured hundreds of his followers. In 1964, as Khomeini continued to oppose the shah's government, he was exiled first to Turkey and then to Iraq.

The shah recognized the importance of Shi'ism, the most important minority sect within Islam and Iran's state religion for nearly five centuries. To gain control over it, he created the Religious Corps. Members of the Religious Corps were graduates of the universities, not the seminaries controlled by the *ulama*. Corpsmen offered a Pahlavi version of Shi'ism. The shah added to this direct challenge to the *ulama* an increasing interest in glorification of pre-Islamic Persia. In 1971 the shah celebrated the 2,500th anniversary of the founding of the Persian Empire by Cyrus the Great. In the ruins of Persepolis he created a tent city with marble bathrooms and other luxurious furnishings. French caterers supplied food and wine. In his speech, the shah seemed to ignore the Islamic heritage in favor of the older Persian connection: "at this moment when Iran renews its pledge to History . . . to watch over your [Cyrus the Great's] glorious heritage. . . ."

Iran's economy grew rapidly in the 1960s and 1970s, fed by the increasing Western need for oil. Economic growth raised the standard of living for many but not all of the population. The *bazaaris*, merchants and shopkeepers who formed the older sector of the middle class, saw their prosperity and influence decline with the influx of foreign goods and the development of Western retail and financial institutions. The newer sectors of the middle class, especially people in the professions, prospered but increasingly began to clamor for greater political participation.

A large working class developed but many were not well paid and lived in urban areas that lacked adequate public facilities. Many others in the countryside found themselves left behind by the changing economy. Like many in the new middle classes, those workers who were relatively well off and accustomed to urban life wanted increased participation in politics.

The dilemma for the shah was how to maintain autocratic power while continuing to develop the country economically and socially. The major problem actually was his failure to see the dilemma clearly. It seemed that nothing could possibly stand in the way of continuing to rule autocratically. The shah enjoyed the unstinting support of the United States, which saw Iran as one of its most important allies in the Cold War. Additionally, the shah could depend on a large, well-equipped military and on the brutal efficiency of SAVAK. Also, he had created opportunities for wealth and power for a relatively small number of supporters.

The shah maintained the façade of parliamentary democracy, creating various political parties that lacked any independence. Both the parliament and the judiciary did what the shah wanted. The constitution of 1906, which limited his powers in theory, was ignored except when it was convenient to adhere to it. In terms of institutions, parties, and associations, there were no outlets for opinions or interests that ran counter to those of the shah.

Opposition to the shah continued, mostly in exile. The older political organizations, the National Front, the Liberation Movement (Islamic and nationalist), and the leftist Tudeh Party, still had representation among Iranian students in Europe and North America. Two guerrilla organizations (the Mojahedin-e Khalq and Fada'iyun-e Khalq) carried out a few operations in the 1970s.

More important than organizations were two leading ideologues. Ali Shariati provided a revolutionary version of Shi'ism, which was Shi'ism as a doctine of liberation. This version was embraced by many secular opposition figures. Khomeini advanced an interpretation of Shi'ism that went in a different direction. In 1969 he declared Islam opposed to the monarchy. Instead, his view was the *ulama* should rule through an Islamic government. A decade later, this was the path the Islamic Revolution took in Iran.

The Islamic Revolution

In the mid-1970s the shah attempted to deal with economic problems caused in large part by a fall in the price of oil. The economic boom, heavily dependent on the sale of oil, ended while inflation took off. The government instituted a number of policies to fight inflation, including the arrest and conviction of several thousand businessmen accused of profiteering, most of them *bazaaris*. Then in 1977, the government imposed a freeze on wages and salaries while increasing taxes. This angered many in the middle class. Finally, many who were dependent on government assistance were hurt by efforts to reduce government expenditures.

The shah turned to political liberalization in an effort to deal with rising popular discontent. Attempts to reform, too late and too limited, opened the way to a growing oppositional movement. The shah was faced with the need either to repress the opposition or to move further in the direction of political reform. Reluctant to make use of the repressive forces he commanded, he failed to see the growing connections between secular and Islamic opposition forces. His hesitation, probably exacerbated by the side effects of treatment for cancer, proved fatal to his regime. Heavily centralized, the regime depended on the direction of the shah to sustain it. American policy in this period also veered between liberalization and tough responses to the Iranian opposition. The opposition sensed the United States no longer backed the shah unconditionally.

Leaders of the National Front and a few intellectuals took advantage of liberalization to circulate open letters complaining about the shah's regime. Professional and student organizations were either revived or created. Instead of working with the largely reformist and secular opposition, the government chose to attack Khomeini in an article in a government newspaper in January 1978. The reaction to the article transformed the protest movement.

At a pro-Khomeini rally in Qom, the center of Shi'i seminaries, police killed a dozen people. Forty days after the killings, the police attempted to stop people in Tabriz from commemorating the deaths of the martyrs of Qom. Several were killed and hundreds arrested. What were intended originally to be peaceful and localized protests became nationwide movements of protest. The *ulama* used their network of mosques and Islamic associations to bring people out for forty-day commemorations. Each commemoration produced more martyrs. The size of the movement and its overtly religious character made it extremely difficult for the regime to combat. Within Iran, Ayatollah Seyyed Kazim Shariatmadari, a vocal critic of the government, assumed a prominent role. Outside Iran, Khomeini quickly assumed a position of leadership.

A mysterious fire in a theater in Abadan in August 1978 that killed some 370 people heightened the tension. The opposition blamed SAVAK for the fire. The shah seemingly had two options at this point. He could use SAVAK to repress the protest movement or he could work with the moderate forces in the opposition, Shariatmadari and the National Front. Instead he ordered the formation of a national unity government in September 1978. The government released some political prisoners, dissolved the Rastakhiz Party (which had been formed as a party loyal to the shah), and reinstated the Islamic calendar. However, the Black Friday massacre in September 1978, during which the police killed hundreds of protesters, ended any chances for cooperation between Shariatmadari and the national unity government.

The Ayatollah Khomeini never indicated any willingness to cooperate. The shah prevailed upon the Iraqi government to expel Khomeini. Nationwide strikes, beginning in the fall of 1978, paralyzed the economy and led to an alliance between the National Front and Khomeini. Nationalists, radicals, and intellectuals believed that Khomeini was a useful unifying symbol and that he would leave politics as soon as the shah abdicated. Khomeini used such themes as independence, freedom, and democracy to unify the protestors. The protest movement circulated cassette tapes of Khomeini's sermons in Iran. It also made use of the newly installed direct dial telephone system to coordinate its activities and stay in contact with Khomeini in exile in France.

The shah's efforts to deal with the revolutionary movement only demonstrated his indecisiveness. In November he ordered the formation of a military government but ordered it to avoid bloodshed. He also read a speech on national television recognizing the legitimacy of the revolutionary movement. By this time demonstrations involving millions of people in Teheran indicated that the shah had little choice but to abdicate. The National Front's Shahpur Bakhtiar agreed to form a government with the proviso that the shah leave Iran.

The United States sent a mission to Iran in January 1979, but it made no effort to try to stop the virtually irresistible popular revolution. The Iranian military also proved ineffective against the revolution. The shah left on 13 January. Khomeini returned in triumph on 1 February and shortly after that formed a provisional revolutionary government under Mehdi Bazargan. For a short time there were two governments. Units of the military briefly resisted, but declared their neutrality on 11 February. Bakhtiar went into hiding. On 1 April 1979, a national referendum in which the only choice was an Islamic Republic led to its establishment. Six months later another national referendum resulted in the approval of an Islamic constitution.

Revolutionary Iran

The seizure of power in 1979 and the approval of an Islamic constitution marked the beginning of a bold experiment in political and social change. Khomeini and his followers created a theocracy. It changed life in Iran in important ways and appeared to presage a far larger movement of Islamic fundamentalism that some observers predicted would lead to a "clash of civilizations."

The Islamic constitution called for an elected parliament composed of people who had first to be approved as good Muslims and supporters of the constitution before they could run for office. It also called for a popularly elected president. Finally, the constitution called for a supreme court, the Council of Guardians. It was to be composed of six clerics, selected by the clergy, and six laymen, selected by the parliament, serving six-year terms. The Council of Guardians ruled on whether acts of government or laws violated the constitution or Islamic law.

Set above the structure of the government was another office, that of the *vilayat-e faqih*, the just Islamic jurist. The first *faqih* was Ayatollah Khomeini.

He could provide advice to the parliament and the president and, if necessary, overrule the government. The creation of this position in particular represented the triumph of Shi'i fundamentalism. It rested in large part on the enormous popularity of Khomeini and the trust that millions of poor and lower middle class Iranians had in him.

Islamic fundamentalism was also organized in the *komitehs* and revolutionary courts that had been established in the course of the revolution, in the Islamic Republic Party (IRP), and in the Islamic Revolutionary Guard, by far the largest militia in revolutionary Iran. A fundamental internal weakness was that many of the *ulama* wanted to maintain existing systems of property and income while many of the revolution's poorer supporters wanted a more equitable distribution of the nation's wealth. The appearance of serious external threats to the revolution in the 1980s temporarily kept this potential source of domestic discord from developing further.

Iranians were well aware of the hostility of the United States toward the Islamic Revolution. When the shah arrived in New York City in October 1979 to seek treatment for his cancer, the assumption of Iranian revolutionaries was that a plot to return the shah to power was underway. The revolutionaries viewed the American embassy in Tehran as a vital center for the plot. On 4 November, some 450 militants seized the embassy, confiscating a large number of documents and taking fifty-three people hostage. They demanded the shah and his assets be returned to Iran before they would agree to release the hostages. The shah's death from cancer in July 1980 removed one issue. The other issue, the assets of the shah, was negotiated successfully over the next few months. Nevertheless, the hostages were not released until the end of President Jimmy Carter's term in office in January 1981. The failure to secure the release of the hostages was a factor in Carter's defeat in the 1980 elections. The fundamentalists may have delayed settlement in order to discredit domestic opponents and to establish Islamic institutions. The impact on American politics might simply have been an additional bonus.

In the midst of the hostage crisis, Iraq invaded Iran in September 1980. Iraq, a much smaller country both in terms of population and territory, believed it could resolve a longstanding territorial dispute in its favor. The dispute concerned control of the Shatt-al-Arab (the Arab River) leading to the Persian Gulf and the province of Khouzestan. The area in dispute contained oil refineries and other facilities. Iraqi President Saddam Hussein probably also worried that Iraqis would respond to Khomeini's call to establish a second Islamic republic in Iraq. Mostly, it was sheer opportunism on the part of Saddam Hussein. He and other Iraqi leaders assumed that Iran's military would be in disarray following the revolution. In any case, Iran would soon run out of spare parts for its military equipment since the United States had banned arms shipments to Iran.

The war helped to unify the Iranian population. The Iranian army and the Islamic Revolutionary Guards, together with Iran's large air force, halted the Iraqi advance. In mid-1982, Iran launched a counterattack with the intent of overthrowing Saddam Hussein. Iraqi forces were much better equipped, thanks to billions of dollars of oil money loaned it by Saudi Arabia and Kuwait, whose monarchs were desperate to destroy the threat posed by the Islamic Republic of Iran. Iran, with its larger population, could sustain a two-to-one margin in casualties. Both nations resorted to increasingly harsh measures. Iraq even used poison gas on Iranian troops.

What was essentially a stalemate continued until mid-1988. By that time each side had lost several hundred thousand men. The war cost the two sides billions of dollars in destroyed equipment and lowered oil revenue. Ayatollah Khomeini finally agreed to negotiate in the summer of 1988. Fighting largely ended at that point, but peace talks did not take place until the summer of 1990. Iraq, under increasing pressure from the United States and other nations after its August invasion of Kuwait, suddenly granted Iran most of what it had wanted in the settlement.

The Iraq–Iran War diverted the course of the revolution for nearly a decade and left the country in poor shape economically. It helped to create a heavily armed and highly aggressive Iraq under Saddam Hussein. The reaction of the United States and its allies in the Middle East to the appearance of an Islamic Republic of Iran failed to destroy the revolutionary regime. Instead, it managed to create a rogue state in Iraq.

Post-Khomeini Iran

Until the very end of his life, Ayatollah Khomeini continued to push for adherence to extreme fundamentalist principles in the Islamic Republic of Iran. In March 1989 he forced the resignation of Ayatollah Hossein Ali Montazeri, previously designated as Khomeini's successor as *faqih*. Montazeri, once a protégé of Khomeini, had been critical of the Islamic Revolution, in particular in connection with its promises to the people. He had also not supported Khomeini's call for the death of Salman Rushdie for writing *The Satanic Verses*, a novel many Muslims considered blasphemous.

Khomeini's death in June 1989 changed little in Iran. Clerics loyal to Khomeini's basic principles continued to control the government. His death, however, did create an opening for a consideration of practical matters in domestic and foreign policy questions that were connected with the more extreme adherence to fundamentalist principles. The day after Khomeini's death, the Assembly of Experts elected Hojatoleslam Ali Khamenei (Hojatoleslam is a religious title, one level below that of Ayatollah), who had been president of Iran the past eight years, as *faqih*. Hojatoleslam Ali Akbar Hashemi Rafsanjani, speaker of the *majles*, was elected president.

During Rafsanjani's two terms as president, he served as a major spokes-man for the Iranian Revolution, in many ways replacing Ayatollah Khomeini as the voice of Islamic fundamentalism. There was at least a partial return to participation in the global economy. The stock exchange re-opened, some nationalized industries were privatized, and foreign investment encouraged. Overall, however, economic performance remained unsatisfactory. Iran was neither fully capitalist nor did it move toward a kind of populist approach to the economy, one that might involve extensive land redistribution.

In 1997 Rafsanjani stepped down, since the constitution limited a president to two terms. Hojatoleslam Mohammad Khatami won the presidential election in 1997. Khatami quickly established a reputation as a political reformer interested in moderating the revolution and working toward a reduction of tensions in the region and normalization of relations with the West. Although Khatami's policies were widely popular in Iran, the conservative clerics under Ayatollah Khamenei have maintained control. Iran remains an Islamic Republic. Khatami was re-elected president in 2001, an indication that strong reformist elements continue to be popular in Iran.

After the 11 September incidents in 2001, President George W. Bush placed Iran in the "Axis of Evil," a grouping that included Iraq and North Korea. Iran, however, despite its past support for Islamic terrorists groups, particularly in Lebanon, does not seem to fit easily into the category of rogue state. However, its continued existence as a revolutionary state based on Islamic fundamentalism makes it suspect to the United States and other nations concerned with terrorist movements that appear tightly connected to various kinds of Islamic extremism.

Islamic fundamentalism

Revolutionary states are always feared by other states even when revolutionary governments show little interest in attempting to export their revolution. In the case of the Islamic Republic of Iran, the record has been mixed. It did call directly for the overthrow of the Iraqi government, but in large part this was in response to the actions of that government toward Iran. Iran also sponsored or sheltered a number of terrorist groups operating primarily in Lebanon on behalf of the Palestinian movement. The various Islamic fundamentalist groups that have appeared in Algeria, Egypt, the Sudan, Afghanistan, Pakistan and elsewhere have little connection with Islamic fundamentalism in Iran and certainly have not been directed or controlled by Iran. For many the appeal of Islamic fundamentalism is that it provides an alternative ideology to the secularism of the West. Since it calls for the integration of Islam not only into political but also into social and cultural concerns, it can be seen as a superior approach to life. It offers a means of struggling against privileged elites, who now can be seen as having sold out to Western interests.

The Taliban in Afghanistan emerged from the chaos of post-Soviet Afghanistan to seize control of Kabul in 1996. After the events of 11 September 2001, the United States' invasion of Afghanistan destroyed the regime and its highly conservative policies. In Algeria the fundamentalists won electoral victories in 1990 but massacred dozens of civilians when the military regime denied them what they had won at the polls. In Egypt, the regime was able to repress the fundamentalists and also appropriate many of the Islamic ideas through social and cultural policies. Elsewhere, in the Sudan, Pakistan, and Turkey, the regimes were able to use Islamic fundamentalism to strengthen their regimes. Only in Afghanistan did anything like a revolutionary Islamic fundamentalism gain full power.

Conclusion

The Iranian Revolution of 1979 furnishes a good example of a revolution brought on by the stresses and strains produced by the efforts of the government to make the country part of the world economy. The same pattern, to a greater or less extent, may be seen in each of the other twentieth-century revolutions examined in this study (Vietnam is something of an exception in that it was initially part of the French colony of Indochina). Attempts to bring the country into the world economy damaged the economic interests of many different groups. In the case of Iran, both the clergy and *bazaaris* found much to dislike with the introduction of Western economic methods and institutions. Landowners and poor peasants also failed to share in the vast new wealth created by oil production in Iran. Many from these same groups were also disturbed by the introduction of Western culture and social practices, as they were not simply unfamiliar but seemingly antithetical to orthodox Islamic practices.

Economic, social, and cultural change in Iran produced several new groups. In particular, a new middle class, well educated and based in the professions, appeared to challenge the older middle class composed of the *bazaaris* and *ulama*. A large urban working class also developed in connection with oil production and other elements of an industrial economy. Both the new middle class and the new urban working class quickly became interested in a more truly democratic political system and disillusioned with the obvious corruption and cronyism that characterized the shah's Iran.

The shah, for his part, failed to recognize the extent to which he had alienated large groups of Iranians and offended religious sensibilities. He also failed to understand the need to maintain the support of the new groups he had done so much to create. He did, of course, face a dilemma. How could he continue to keep his powerful supporters in his family, in the government, army, and the SAVAK satisfied and still move toward a more open society, one in which political parties and interest groups were free to establish themselves and compete in the marketplace of ideas? Even with astute advisors, as was the case in the Russian Empire before World War I, it is difficult for an autocrat to relinquish power, especially in a gradual and controlled manner. It is a balancing act only a rare leader could attempt successfully. The shah, like Nicholas II before him, was fundamentally a weak and indecisive person, not capable of mastering a situation such as he found himself in during the 1970s.

The revolution was initially composed of many different kinds of oppositional figures: nationalists, democrats, leftist intellectuals, and Islamic fundamentalists. The Ayatollah Khomeini, a man of firm principles and great courage, captured the imagination of secular and religious revolutionaries alike. He was the charismatic figure with a vision of an Islamic Republic that seemed completely unlikely ever to be realized, even after the shah fled the country. Of course, Khomeini had more than charisma. He also had organization, an existing religious network under the control of the *ulama*, and the *komitehs* that they often were responsible for founding. Khomeini added to these assets a powerful political party and a large militia. The secular revolutionaries, badly divided along several political lines, could not compete. They generally had no way to reach large groups of people, much less gain their loyalty and support.

The Iranian Revolution changed Iran with breathtaking speed, introducing a theocratic political system, a legal system based on the *shari'a*, and a series of ideas about society and culture that undid many of the shah's changes over the previous three decades. In particular, the revolution brought about significant change in the possibilities for women, changes symbolized by the new dress code. Censorship was imposed on newspapers and other publications. Intellectuals found there were clear limits to what they could investigate, say, or write. The revolutionary regime engaged in a kind of post-revolutionary terror in 1979, arresting thousands, and torturing and executing hundreds. The war with Iraq brought with it a strict conformity but also a kind of revolutionary unity.

It remains to be seen exactly what direction the Iranian Revolution will take in the future. Although it may be uncomfortable for the many who enjoyed aspects of the shah's Iran and who might want to return to secular politics and a more open society and culture, the revolution has loosened to the point where there can be some discussion and people who disagree with the fundamentalist direction can still be elected. Early in the twenty-first century, the Islamic Republic of Iran remains a disappointment to millions of Iranians, a repressive regime that has not yet been able to improve the quality of life for many Iranians, whether in the cities or in the countryside. As is the case in Vietnam, an entire generation has appeared that knows little about Iran under the shah and is attracted to much that is characteristic of the West. The role of Islam is being openly questioned in Iran. It does not appear that there will be a popular uprising against the Islamic government in the near future. Nonetheless, questions continue and less and less genuine support seems likely.

Iran has great potential both in terms of an increased standard of living for much of its population and in terms of the important role that it might play regionally. The possibility of a prosperous, democratic, and regionally influential Iran that is simultaneously heavily influenced by Islam is an attractive one. The idea of a just and free society based on Islam was the original goal of the revolution. The revolution has failed to achieve that goal, but achieving it at some point in the future is not out of the question.

Further reading

Abrahamian, Ervand (1982) *Iran: Between Two Revolutions*. Princeton, NJ: Princeton University Press.

Afary, Janet (1996) *The Iranian Constitutional Revolution, 1906–1911: Grassroots Democracy, Social Democracy, and the Origins of Feminism*. New York: Columbia University Press.

Bayat, Mangol (1991) *Iran's First Revolution: Shi'ism and the Constitutional Revolution of 1905–1909*. New York: Oxford University Press.

Brumbert, Daniel (2001) *Reinventing Khomeini: The Struggle for Reform in Iran*. Chicago: University of Chicago Press.

Eickelman, Dale and Piscatori, James (1996) *Muslim Politics*. Princeton, NJ: Princeton University Press.

Keddie, Nikki R. with Richards, Yann (1981) *Roots of Revolution: An Interpretive History of Modern Iran*. New Haven, CT: Yale University Press.

Kinzer, Stephen (2003) *All the Shah's Men: An American Coup and the Roots of the Middle East Terror*, Hoboken, NJ: John Wiley & Sons.

Mohsen, Milani M. (1988) *The Making of Iran's Islamic Revolution: From Monarchy to Islamic Republic*, second edition. Boulder, CO: Westview Press.

Sciolino, Elaine (2000) *Persian Mirrors: The Elusive Face of Iran*. New York: Free Press.

Wright, Robin (2000) *The Last Great Revolution: Turmoil and Transformation in Iran*. New York: Knopf.

Chapter 7

Revolutions in world history

The title of Chapter 1, "Bringing revolutions back into history," was meant to suggest two basic ideas. One idea asserts that revolutions had histories and that approaching them with historical methods would pay sizeable dividends. This is not to say that political scientists, sociologists, and others from the social sciences had nothing to contribute, only to indicate that we must not confine ourselves to typologies, etiologies, and overarching patterns. A second, far larger idea involved pointing out the importance of revolutions in world history over the past four centuries, at least since the British Revolution of the seventeenth century. Revolutions are not diseases that had to run their course or disruptions to a state of desired equilibrium that had to be dealt with before the continuity of history might be resumed. They are integral parts of the historical record, one way of solving problems, one way of deciding which groups pay what price for whatever happens.

To put the matter somewhat differently, the phenomenon of revolution has been and likely will continue to be a potent factor in shaping the raw material of history. From that it follows that any attempt to set down the historical record that regards revolution as an interruption to the flow of history or an anomaly will be a flawed attempt. Revolution as we have come to understand it in the last few centuries has done more than contribute drama and bloodshed to history. It has been a major part of that history, in the same way as industrialization or urbanization. It has also played a major role in the sense that human beings often acted in certain ways to pre-empt it or to dampen down situations that looked likely to flare up.

Revolution as politics (I)

Politics has always included the threat or use of violence and force. From the seventeenth century to the present, in an increasingly self-conscious way, political actors came to recognize revolution as another way to doing politics.

The original intention in seventeenth-century Britain was conservation of political institutions, rights, and customs. The mixture of political and religious concerns, however, in the context of rapidly changing social and economic circumstances, took those involved in the events of the 1640s far beyond their original intentions. And it also produced a variety of highly radical proposals from fringe groups.

Once the revolutionaries had executed Charles I, they did not seek to install a new king or to establish a new dynasty but rather sought, somewhat ineffectually, to construct a new system of government based on national sovereignty and popular representation. They did not succeed in this. The end result of the mid-century British Revolution was a dictatorship. After the death of Oliver Cromwell, the English preferred the restoration of the Stuart dynasty in the person of Charles II to the vagaries of continued dictatorship. Certain limitations on the power of the Crown remained nonetheless. When James II mismanaged the political situation in England in the 1680s, these limitations were made explicit in the arrangements that brought William and Mary to the throne. It marked the beginnings of a long, largely successful process of modifying a system of constitutional monarchy.

Without meaning to do so, the British began the construction of a tradition of revolution that would spread throughout the world over the next three centuries. In the context of the eighteenth-century Enlightenment, the British achievements of broad political participation, limits on the authority of the crown, and an open society that recognized merit as well as rewarded privilege caught the attention of many who considered themselves part of the international intellectual and cultural movement of the Enlightenment. In a broader way, the Enlightenment itself contributed to the beginnings of a tradition of revolution because it emphasized the possibility of understanding political and economic processes and attempted to reform existing institutions and customs along the lines of those understandings. Change was possible, in fact desirable. Resistance to reform was also possible, and revolution came to be one response to regimes that stifled change and reform.

It was the French who established the idea that politics could be carried on through revolutionary means, and might best be carried on in this way. By the late eighteenth century the British had all but forgotten the revolutionary origins of the system of constitutional monarchy they were still engaged in modifying. Observers largely dismissed the American Revolution as a political anomaly: of course, one might create a quite different system in the New World where customs, traditions, and long-established institutions had no purchase.

At the beginning of the French Revolution, no one was thinking in terms of a radical rearrangement of the political system. The French state needed new sources of revenue. French political actors, particularly those drawn from the aristocracy, were willing to agree to new forms of taxation in exchange for increased influence in political affairs. It was hardly a new discussion, more a new opportunity for political bargaining. The circumstances prevailing in the summer of 1789, however, pushed the French both to acts of symbolic violence such as the storming of the Bastille and to radical universal statements such as the "Declaration of the Rights of Man and Citizen." By 1794, under the pressure of invading armies and bands of counter-revolutionaries, France had moved to a bold experiment meant not simply to rearrange political forms but also to create revolutionaries, new men and women living in a different and supposedly far better society. From this point on, although feared perhaps even more than desired, the idea reigned that revolutionary politics was a more expeditious way of achieving political goals. In the nineteenth and twentieth centuries there was no question that revolution was an alternate way of doing politics.

Two other points might be made about revolution as another way of doing politics. First, revolutions produce a kind of demonstration effect, i.e. a revolution in one state may cause other states to take action to prevent the outbreak of revolution. Most frequently, this is in the form of counter-revolutionary activities, whether directed toward the population of the state fearful of revolutionary contagion, as in the case of Catherine the Great's Russia in the 1790s, or against the revolutionary state itself. In other cases, however, it may lead to reform within the state in an attempt to head off the possibility of revolutionary change. One of the great ironies of Marxism is that Karl Marx and Friedrich Engels failed to see that other observers could do what they had done, determine the existence of certain trends in contemporary life and take action in response. Europeans in the second half of the nineteenth century paid at least minimal attention to social and economic issues, sponsoring reforms that gave many in the working classes the idea it would be better to work with the existing system than to try to overthrow it. In any case, after the revolutions of 1848, the middle class, having noted the dangerous unpredictability of revolution, mostly opted for gradual change.

Secondly, revolutions have sometimes come in waves, generally because similar circumstances elsewhere often elicit the same kinds of reactions as in the original locus of revolution. Thus in 1830, and especially in 1848, revolutions broke out in several areas in Europe that sought unification and independence and/or political change in the direction of constitutionalism and representative government. In the first decade of the twentieth century several states underwent revolution in response to domestic interest in constitutions and parliaments and to the external pressures of the international economy. After World War II a series of national liberation movements frequently resorted to revolutionary violence. It is worth noting, however, that by the twentieth century, revolutions that were broadly similar, such as those in China, Mexico, Russia, and Persia, differed in detail because of the vastly different geographical and cultural bases for each revolution. Nonetheless, both the Russian and the Chinese Revolutions were widely imitated in the twentieth century. By the post-World War II period, observers of all kinds sought to isolate the "lessons" of different revolutions, some in order to prevent them, others in the hopes of imitating a successful revolution.

Origins

In tracing the origins of revolutions, we have emphasized regime failure. Dictatorial or autocratic regimes cannot be maintained by the use of force alone. There must be a semblance of legitimacy and various powerful groups must have a reason to accept and support the regime. Either that or they will find reasons to go against it. Even in an autocracy, politics depends on the construction and maintenance of a political coalition. Sometimes regimes flounder when they become so conspicuously rapacious that they drive almost all of their supporters into the opposition. Good examples of this might be Batista's Cuba or Somoza's Nicaragua. Generally, however, regimes have difficulty managing rapidly changing economic circumstances or in keeping changes in the political system in line with social, economic, and cultural change. The shah's Iran in the 1970s is a good example of this kind of situation. Often, regimes attempt reform and change, but only succeed in encouraging revolution. Once they themselves question the legitimacy of the old system, it is difficult to maneuver rapidly and carefully enough to avoid a collapse of the system.

War can also destabilize a regime. Such was the case for the Russian Empire in World War I, but, interestingly enough, not the case for the German Empire, which transformed itself imperfectly into the Weimar Republic after the war. World War II left many colonial powers unable to maintain control of their empires and created conditions favorable to revolution or at least to armed struggle.

Once the old political system and all that goes with it begins to break down, a flood of grievances and suppressed aspirations overwhelms the political scene. It is more or less the same phenomenon as a dam giving way. What has been contained and channeled now surges across the landscape, often in a very destructive way. The range of ideas, schemes, and theories produced by the British Revolution of the mid-seventeenth century is a good example of this. Another example is the Soviet Union in the 1920s, a period when cranks, geniuses, and bureaucrats vied with one another for the scarce resources available to them. The early days of a revolution are perhaps the most interesting, simply because practically anything, no matter how utopian, seems possible.

Almost all the revolutions discussed in this book have featured secular ideologies. By the early nineteenth century several seemingly unrelated ideas of what revolution might do co-existed. They ranged from liberal ideas about politics to socialist ideas about economic change and reform. At the far reaches of socialist thought were discussions of human nature and how best to structure society to allow humanity to develop as fully as possible. This, in essence, was the direction taken by the early Marx and Engels, a direction they never relinquished even if it was gradually lost in the actual efforts to establish Marxist regimes. Other ideas about revolution concerned the possibility of using revolution to unify and liberate areas that did not yet have a national existence. Among those areas were what had been Poland and what would become Italy and Germany.

Out of what some have termed the "ferment of discussion" between 1815 and 1848 came the powerful theory put forth by Karl Marx and Friedrich Engels. Marxism, particularly as revised in the twentieth century by Lenin, Stalin, Mao, and others, became the ideology of choice. In many cases, of course, the various strands of revolutionary ideology intertwined. One might point to Ho Chi Minh's revolutionary declaration on 2 September 1945 in Hanoi, a statement that quoted both Thomas Jefferson and the authors of the "Declaration of the Rights of Man and Citizen." That Ho also intended to bring about a social revolution based on Marxist teachings was, however, not brought to the fore. Instead, he emphasized themes that the Americans present that day might respond to and similar themes that the French, not yet returned to their old colony, would have to consider in dealing with Ho's audacious move.

Although secular ideologies dominated the nineteenth and twentieth centuries and became in many ways highly similar to religions in terms of high priests, sacred writings, a series of sacraments, and other features one associates with religion, religion as such also played an important role in the revolutions under discussion. The British Revolution of the mid-seventeenth century is a mixed case in that religious concerns at that time so easily spilled over into political concerns. Control of the political institutions was crucial in that political decisions could and often did vitally affect religious interests. By the same token, religious considerations might result in people making political decisions, alliances with Catholic powers, for example, with far-reaching consequences.

The Mexican Revolution contained a streak of virulent anti-clericalism. The Catholic Church in Mexico was seen as an agent of obscurantism and an obstacle to progress. In the 1920s, the Cristero Rebellion was an attempt by a portion of Mexican Catholics to counter the damage done to church interests by the revolutionary state. The revolutionary state in the Soviet Union was even more firmly anti-clerical. With the exception of World War II, when the party and government solicited the support of the Russian Orthodox Church in the Great Fatherland War against Nazi Germany, the Soviet establishment actively persecuted not only the Russian Orthodox faithful but also other adherents of Christian faiths. It also worked against adherents of the Jewish and Islamic religions.

In Vietnam the situation was complicated by the powerful influence of Vietnamese Catholics who had come south after the 1954 settlement at Geneva. They constituted a major power bloc in the Republic of South Vietnam, especially under Ngo Dinh Diem. Protests by the Buddhist community in South Vietnam led indirectly to the overthrown and assassination of Diem in 1963. Both the Vietminh and the Viet Cong professed views that accorded better with Confucian principles than anything put forth by the

South Vietnamese state. Once the Communists came to power, however, they frequently persecuted organized religions.

Only in Iran did religion ultimately furnish the basis for a revolutionary ideology. Iran was heavily influenced by Western liberal ideas about politics and nationalism. It had also long been exposed to Marxist ideas as well. Islamic fundamentalism, however, furnished what appeared to be a much more satisfactory approach to revolutionary politics than liberal or Marxist ideas. Islamic fundamentalism continues to furnish a basis for several revolutionary movements. It has, however, proved to be problematic in the actual governing of a state. The most useful relationship of Islamic clergy to the political and juridical systems has yet to be determined.

The role of the charismatic leader has already been discussed in great detail. It is, perhaps, enough to note here how seldom charismatic leaders seemed charismatic in the more conventional sense. Few would have fit the current idea of a telegenic political personality, a Tony Blair or a George W. Bush. It is perhaps best to see the revolutionary leaders presented in previous chapters, Cromwell, Zapata, Villa, Lenin, Stalin, Ho, Giap, and Khomeini, as people with both vision and determination.

However, are the people who carry out the revolution and seize power the best suited to exercise that power? The record is mixed and tantalizingly incomplete. Lazaro Cardenas seemed to be exactly the person needed to follow up the accomplishments of the Mexican Revolution, but his successors proved to be people capable mostly of cynical arrangements for the sharing of power and wealth. Lenin gave some evidence in his last years that he might have the patience and wisdom to transform the Soviet Union slowly and carefully. His untimely death left the question of who the real Lenin was, the ruthless Lenin of 1917 and the Civil War or the more patient Lenin of the NEP, unanswered. Also, what would have happened had the elections scheduled in 1956 for Vietnam been carried out? Ho, who certainly would have won them, might have had a chance to exercise his apparent tendency toward patient, pragmatic, and moderate approaches to the use of power. Instead, the two parts of Vietnam spiraled toward an armed struggle that would leave the nation united but exhausted nearly twenty years later.

External factors are clearly important for a complete understanding of why revolutions begin and take the shape they do. The British Revolution of the mid-seventeenth century was allowed to play itself out with relatively little outside interference from the continent, although, of course, events in Ireland and Scotland were often decisive. The Revolution of 1688, however, owed much to external factors. Would William have landed an expeditionary force if Louis XIV had kept his forces close to the Dutch borders? The Mexican Revolution took several turns because of blatant American interference. The Russian Revolution, even before the Cold War proper, was heavily influenced by the hostility of various great powers. Vietnam, of course, is the prime example of an area deeply influenced by the needs and intentions of other countries. First France and then the United States sought to determine its destiny. Even its nominal allies, the Soviet Union and China, followed their own particular interests on many occasions, much to the detriment of Vietnam. Finally, Iran and its revolution, in so many ways a product of the Cold War, have continued to struggle with a regional situation that, primarily because of oil resources but also because of the Israeli–Palestinian question, has attracted the ongoing attention of many powerful nations.

Revolution as politics (II)

We come back then to the idea of revolution as another form of politics. Revolutionaries take on new interest once they have gained power. What will they do with this power and, ultimately, will the revolution succeed or fail? It is not enough to trace the origins of revolution to the point of seizing power. To be sure, in the second half of the twentieth century, a cottage industry developed, particularly among political scientists, that concerned itself primarily with the etiology of revolution in the hopes of eliminating conditions favorable to revolution or stopping if it should break out nonetheless. Whatever the value of this exercise (and it could have been valuable if such knowledge had been used to institute reform), it resulted in partial, even distorted, conceptions of revolution. What happens after the seizure of power, how that power is consolidated and used, is certainly as important, perhaps more important, than how power was seized in the first place.

Because it is so important to see how power is used and the extent to which the revolution lives up to its ideals and goals, this book has pursued the stories of various revolutions long past the point where most other studies end. It has attempted to find either where the revolution has "died," embalmed as it were in rhetoric and symbol, or at least has fallen back into a more conventional kind of politics in which revolutionary origins, if recognized at all, are only given the occasional ceremonial nod. Thus the French in celebrating the bicentennial of the French Revolution could assure themselves that the revolution was now truly over, whether that was so or not.

Sometimes, as in the United States in the 1960s, a revolution, long remembered as myths about the Founding Fathers or fireworks on the 4th of July, returns. In this case, the Civil Rights Movement, especially as expressed in Martin Luther King, Jr.'s "I Have a Dream" speech from 1963, recalled to Americans the unfinished business from the American Revolution and from the Civil War and Reconstruction. It set off waves of change not only for African-Americans but also for women, Latinos/as, Asian-Americans, gays, and others.

In the case of the revolutions discussed in this book, the British Revolution probably ended with the Reform Bill of 1832, which established the primacy of the House of Commons in the British parliamentary system. The British, perhaps because of the American and French Revolutions, tended to confine recognition of their revolutionary origins to the Glorious Revolution of 1688. Emphasis was and has continued to be placed on the gradualist and moderate nature of the British political system, overlooking the contentious nature of the eighteenth and early nineteenth centuries.

The Mexican Revolution effectively ended with the end of the presidency of Lazaro Cardenas. It managed to maintain itself, largely as rhetoric and occasional gesture, for another sixty years. It became, as some scholars termed it, the "Frozen Revolution." In a sense, the entire revolution, and not just the great leader, was embalmed and placed on display. The most important legacy from the revolution, the idea of what it is to be Mexican, may help in future efforts to provide Mexico with a political system that can make the most of that country's considerable social, economic, and cultural potential.

The Russian Revolution began to flounder at almost the same time the Mexican Revolution first ran into serious problems, in the 1970s. Leonid Brezhnev, the General Secretary of the Communist Party in the period, became a personification of the problems of the revolution. As he aged, he grew increasingly weak, ill, and senile. The next two party leaders, Yuri Andropov and Konstantin Chernenko, had only short terms in office. Mikhail Gorbachev, the last communist leader and a believer in the system, brought new energy and intelligence to the struggle to make Communism relevant, but by then it was much too late. Given the weight of the Stalinist legacy, with its emphasis on heavy industry, military preparation, and conformity, it might already have been too late when Stalin died in 1953.

The Vietnamese and the Iranian revolutionaries have both been in power for approximately the same length of time. Both have endured long years as pariah nations, at least so far as the United States and its allies are concerned. Otherwise, circumstances differ considerably. The Socialist Republic of Vietnam came into being in 1975 after thirty years of war. It faced not only the need to reconstruct a country devastated by fighting but also the need to reconcile two rather different regions, the north and the south. Heavily influenced by Maoist ideas imported from the People's Republic of China, it was not well equipped to deal with the array of problems it faced. Although the introduction of *doi moi* (renovation) in the 1980s and considerable foreign investment in the 1990s led to some improvements in the economy, the bureaucrats of the party, government, and military continue to stand in the way of rapid reconstruction. A new generation, born since 1975 and knowing little of the long struggle for independence and unification, will almost certainly bring significant change in the next couple of decades. In Vietnam there will be a struggle to define the revolution and find a political system that can incorporate its legacy and still allow Vietnam to participate in the global economy.

Iran should be in far better shape than Vietnam as it faces the future. Although it had a terrible legacy of war from the Iraq–Iran War of the 1980s, it possessed a basic industrial and commercial infrastructure at the beginning

of the 1990s and impressive oil production resources. The Islamic fundamentalism that still directs Iranian politics and life presents the same kind of
obstacle to pragmatic development of political and economic arrangements as
does the Marxism of Vietnam. Islam, as one of the great religious traditions of
the world, has far more to offer than Marxism in terms of guidelines for living
one's life. The question nonetheless remains as to how much influence Islamic
clerics should have in the working of basic political and economic systems. As
in Vietnam, the new generation of Iranians (in this case born after 1979) is
increasingly impatient with the failure of the government to deal with pressing
economic and social issues. There will also be a struggle in Iran over the next
few decades to define the revolution and find a way to fit it into a polity that
can answer the questions now being raised. In Iran's case, though, there are
many resources available for the work of reconstruction and development.
Vietnam has fewer resources and a much heavier burden of historical tragedy
to bear.

Finally, a few comments on the revolutions of 1989 in Eastern Europe,
particularly those in Czechoslovakia and the German Democratic Republic,
will work to conclude this section and introduce the next. The events of the
fall of 1989 surprised nearly all observers. Somehow, large numbers of brave,
determined, and resourceful people gathered together first in Leipzig in the
GDR, then in other cities around the country. A little later that fall a similar
phenomenon took place in Prague. Both regimes were knocked off balance
and never recovered.

The situation was particularly interesting in the GDR. In the first part of
1990 the revolutionary coalition in power moved rapidly toward amalgamation
with the Federal Republic of Germany (critics insisted it was a case of the FRG
"annexing" the GDR). In this case, revolutionaries used power to become part
of a system they regarded as successful and attractive. Czechoslovakia had no
neighboring country to amalgamate with (and in fact soon underwent the
"Velvet Divorce" that split it into the Czech Republic and the Slovak
Republic). Nonetheless, it, too, used power to move as rapidly as possible
toward representative democracy and industrial capitalism. These were seen as
central characteristics of a successful polity and economy.

Some commentators have expressed doubts that the events of 1989 were
truly revolutions. Still, an adequate definition of revolution is the replacement
of one system by another and that was what happened in 1989. If, when
revolutionaries did away with the old communist system, they adopted an
already existing democratic, free enterprise system, were their actions any
less revolutionary for that? Whether the revolutions of 1989 were "successful"
or not is another, often difficult to answer, question. Certainly in what was once
the German Democratic Republic, many would question the idea of success
while others would confirm it.

"Success" or "failure"?

The most difficult question the book raises is this: what exactly constitutes "success" and "failure" in revolution? We have insisted that it must be more than the seizure of power. Any judgment of a revolution must rest on the uses made of power. "Success," as noted in the first chapter, involves three criteria. A successful revolution should: (1) provide for individual liberty; (2) result in a flexible and open political system that can deal with economic, social, and cultural changes; and (3) generate improvement in the well-being of those it affects. By these criteria, only the British Revolution of the seventeenth century may be considered successful. Mexico and Russia, now that they have moved away from the restrictions imposed by their revolutionary regimes, have the opportunity to become successful. Vietnam and Iran seem unlikely to achieve success in the near term.

If we take a long view, many revolutions that did not seem successful initially might eventually be viewed as successful. The British Revolution of the mid-seventeenth century was not successful in that the Stuart dynasty was restored and much that had characterized Cromwell's regime was undone. The Revolution of 1688, however, seemed to confirm that at least some of the political changes brought about earlier – a constitutional monarchy, guarantees of rights, and so forth – and certainly the evolution of the British political system over the next two centuries led to a stable, functional, if still imperfect political arrangement with all kinds of generally useful economic, social, and cultural implications.

The Mexican Revolution was successful in its own, narrow, terms for a generation or so, but the revolution seems to have turned away from itself in 1940 in favor of deals and arrangements that benefited the few at the expense of the many. Early in the twenty-first century it is possible to see that some parts of the revolution might be salvaged, such as the emphasis on national sovereignty and pride in Mexico's Indian past, for example. Much of the revolution will need to be reworked in coming decades.

The Russian Revolution was successful in creating a great power that not only contributed enormously to the defeat of Nazi Germany but also competed successfully with the United States in the Cold War for several decades after the end of World War II. But this was at great cost to Soviet society. The structures that allowed the Soviet Union to function as a great power were insufficiently flexible to allow it to change as rapidly as other states did in the 1960s and 1970s. Despite all the efforts of Mikhail Gorbachev to find a way to keep the communist experiment going, it collapsed in 1991. Now, more than a decade later, the Russian Republic and other successor states are still trying to come to terms with the revolutionary legacy.

In the case of Vietnam and Iran, it is perhaps too soon to know whether their revolutions may be judged as successes or as failures. Vietnam successfully gained independence, but at a terrible cost. Many Vietnamese, particularly those in the south, began to see in the 1960s the terrible destructiveness of the efforts to maintain an independent South Vietnam. The United States must shoulder the responsibility for not allowing Vietnamese leaders in the south to establish a neutral South Vietnam. Some evidence indicates North Vietnam would have allowed a "decent interval" before completing the unification of the country. Unification under conditions different from those prevailing in 1975, i.e. the result of negotiations, might have resulted in a different approach to political and economic affairs than was the case. This is speculation, of course, and everything is naturally much clearer in hindsight than it was at the time.

Iran, as indicated earlier, may yet find a way to combine Islamic guidelines with political and juridical institutions in such a way that the basic political, social, and economic problems of that country can be addressed. A hundred years from now it might be possible to assert that the Vietnamese Revolution "failed" but that the Iranian Revolution "succeeded." After all, it took the French two centuries to decide that their revolution had played itself out. Americans, much to their surprise, found themselves two centuries after their revolution, still working on some of the unresolved questions from that event.

Conclusion

It is possible we now live in a period similar to that of the 1890s. In that period, violence and terrorism were prevalent, as were assassinations, large-scale strikes, and much talk of revolutionary change. Yet it also seemed that a consensus had formed that the use of revolution was a crude and unpredictable way to practice politics. Many looked to reform and gradual change as the means by which to accomplish worthy and necessary goals. This consensus notwithstanding, the early twentieth century was filled with revolutions in every quarter of the globe.

What we cannot predict is when individuals or groups might see in revolution a useful political tool, and when they might use it. No one anticipated the collapse of the East European communist regimes in 1989. As one regime after another lost the capacity to deal with the problems of the day, people took to the streets in numbers so large that the regimes faced the dilemma of massive repression or total inaction, both of which would cast doubt on their legitimacy. Fortunately, with the exception of the rulers of Romania, communist leaders through Eastern Europe lost their resolve and soon lost their power as well.

The conduct of human affairs always has a cost that must be paid one way or another. This cost may be paid in a more or less equitable way. When individuals and groups pay far more than is their share, which is the case still in many parts of the world, it does not necessarily mean that revolution will occur. Many factors enter into the making of a revolution, perhaps the most important being the capacity of a regime to govern. It may govern in a repressive and unjust way, but if it is sufficiently astute and attentive to the interests of a few powerful groups it may well survive. And, of course, it may govern badly but not face determined and visionary opposition or powerful ideologies, thus dodging the revolutionary bullet in another way.

History is a complicated process. It does not necessarily lead to progress or to justice. Revolution, like other forms of politics, is a response to this fundamental situation. Having witnessed its development as a political tool over four centuries, we must acknowledge its existence and recognize that it may, and in many cases should, appear at almost any moment in almost any location.

Further reading

Billington, James H. (1980) *Fire in the Minds of Men: Origins of the Revolutionary Faith*. New York: Basic Books.

Brinton, Crane (1965) *The Anatomy of Revolution*, revised and expanded edition. New York: Random House. First published in 1938.

Dunn, John (1972) *Modern Revolutions: An Introduction to the Analysis of a Political Phenomenon*. Cambridge: Cambridge University Press.

Goldstone, Jack A. (1991) *Revolution and Rebellion in the Early Modern World*. Berkeley and Los Angeles: University of California Press.

—— (editor) (1998) *The Encyclopedia of Political Revolutions*. Washington, DC: Congressional Quarterly Inc.

Goodwin, Jeff (2001) *No Other Way Out: States and Revolutionary Movements, 1945–1991*. Cambridge: Cambridge University Press.

Moore, Barrington, Jr. (1966) *Social Origins of Dictatorship and Democracy: Lord and Peasant in the Making of the Modern World*. Boston: Beacon Press.

Paige, Jeffery M. (1975) *Agrarian Revolution: Social Movements and Export Agriculture in the Underdeveloped World*. New York: Free Press.

Skocpol, Theda (1979) *States and Social Revolutions: A Comparative Analysis of France, Russia, and China*. Cambridge: Cambridge University Press.

Tilly, Charles (1978) *From Mobilization to Revolution*. Reading, MA: Addison-Wesley.

—— (1993) *European Revolutions, 1492–1992*. Oxford: Blackwell.

Creveld, Martin Van (editor) (1996) *The Encyclopedia of Revolutions and Revolutionaries: From Anarchism to Zhou Enlai*. New York: Facts on File.

Index

CPSIA information can be obtained at www.ICGtesting.com
Printed in the USA
LVOW090621040812

292875LV00002B/52/P